TEARS AND BONES

Eight Years Fighting Anorexia

Oihana Bachelet

TEARS AND BONES

Eight Years Fighting Anorexia

Afterwords by Dr Alice Letessier
and Dr Virginie Robert

Max Milo

www.maxmilo.com
ISBN : 978-231502-692-0

I dedicate this book
to my wonderful parents.

Author's Note

This book is aimed at those close to people with eating disorders, those who wish to understand some of the mechanisms of these disorders, and anyone who suffers or has suffered from conflicting relationships with food.

The story begins in 2012, and the treatment of eating disorders may have evolved since then.

It is important to point out that this book recounts a personal and subjective experience, which does not aim to generalize, but to bear witness.

Above all, through the ending of this story, I would like to give hope to people suffering from eating disorders, and to those close to them.

Finally, I would like to warn you that some passages in this book contain descriptions that may be offensive to people affected by eating disorders, depression and suicidal thoughts.

If you are concerned by these issues, I urge you to read this book with caution, and even to postpone it if you fear that certain passages may affect you.

Don't hesitate to talk to your loved ones or healthcare professionals about your difficulties. And, above all, take care of yourself.

The Smell of Lavender

February 2013, Age 12

My bones bang against the sides of the bathtub. The scalding water coats my carcass.

How long have I been here?

I can barely keep my eyes open, the steam is so thick and dense. Everything fades away and floats around me. My knees protrude slightly from the surface of the water, cold, emaciated, covered in bruises. I can barely move them. The scent of lavender wafts through my nostrils from the bath. Maybe that's what death smells like.

A slamming door wakes me. My mother enters the room.

"I'll leave the scale next door... You need to weigh yourself on the way out, okay? Call me when it's right."

I slowly extract myself from the bathtub and step, one foot at a time, onto the bathroom scale. For the first time, it shows a figure under 40 kg: 39.1 kg. My mom looks down. I can no longer express or feel anything. A deep silence builds a wall between her and me. Even *The Voice* keeps a low profile.

My mother leaves the room, leaving me alone in the bathroom, facing the mirror.

I slowly approach my reflection and plunge my eyes into those of the being facing me. I look at my naked, hollowed-out child's torso, my dry, nervous belly, my stunted arms. Then I slowly direct my hands towards my face, and begin to explore it with my fingertips. I furrow the ridge of my prominent cheekbones, the curves of my sunken temples, the volumes of my jaw. The vision of a human skull takes shape in my head.

This is it, I've gone too far. I'll have to leave the house.

The Land

August 2012, 12 years 7 months earlier

Blood flows between my legs. My body disgusts me, everything that forms it and everything that comes out of it. I've gained weight, I notice when I press my fat thighs, flattened on the toilet rim. The skin of my belly is plump and shiny.

I grab some paper towels and stuff them into my panties. I don't dare tell my grandmother I'm having my period for the first time.

My parents aren't home. They're repainting the shutters of our house in the south of France, while my two brothers and I are enjoying a week's vacation in Normandy, at our grandparents' side.

I use the time to prepare for the finals of my department's basketball selections. At the start, there were a lot of us, but now there are only twenty. The selectors will keep fifteen players at the end of the summer.

I've already done two training camps to reach this final stage. The first was in the spring, the second in June and the last will be in a week's time, at the end of August. I know the nineteen girls who will be with me. They're all slim and muscular. Their hair is done up in buns—like dancers. I'd like to be like them. They're very close-knit, because they're almost all from the same club, renowned for its very high standards. It's hard for me to fit in with them.

I'm afraid of disappointing my father and the basketball coach of my village team, who both believe in me.

I train hard to keep up. Every day, I run around the soccer stadium that runs alongside the garden of my grandparents' house. Three laps of the pitch, alternating slow and fast running sequences, to get my heart, muscles and breath used to the changes in pace. My father taught me this method, which is called split training. Then I do a few exercises on the outdoor basketball court.

Fifteen free throws, fifteen straight lay-ups, fifteen push-ups, fifteen lay-backs.

Throughout the workout, I can feel my thighs rubbing together and my body dripping with sweat. I wonder if it's normal to have thighs that touch at 12.

My little brother joins me on the basketball court. He's a year younger than me, athletic and slim. I admire his tapered legs and wish I had the same body shape as him. When we were little, we weighed the same and were the same height. Adults often thought we were twins. I loved those days when we were one. We played together all day long, inventing wonderful worlds and stories of all kinds. We had so much fun. At the start of the school year, my little brother joined me at college, entering 6th and I 5th. My older brother will be leaving middle school and moving on to high school.

"Can you pass the ball to me?" my little brother, Unai, asks me with the look of a laughing child.

I smile and throw the ball across the pitch for him to run after. We burst out laughing.

Sunset looms behind the soccer stadium hedges. A warm breeze caresses my shoulders. The sky turns pink and the laughter of children playing in the distance echoes through the village streets. I love this end-of-summer atmosphere, I wish it would never end.

It's time to head home, as the aperitif approaches. We hurry home with my little brother, happy to share this pleasant moment with our grandparents. My grandpa tells jokes and my grandma listens to us talk. My big brother is there too, having stayed home to watch sports on TV.

My grandmother prepares the aperitif tray, and I can see in her eyes how happy she is to see us all together. My grandfather pours us a glass of orgeat syrup and we cheerfully toast. My attention soon turns to the multitude of savory delights on the table. I peck at them several times and struggle not to give in to temptation any further.

For some time now, an irresistible urge has been driving me to eat frantically. Hearty meals calm me down. At the table, I eat one piece of bread after another. I love the caramelized smell of the crust and the elastic texture of the crumb. And since dinners are light at my grandparents,' I try to compensate.

My grandmother meets my gaze as I reach for the basket again. "You should be careful not to eat too much bread, young girls have to eat less than men."

Looking back, I'm convinced that this advice was meant to be benevolent, like every bit of attention she always paid to my brothers and me. At the age of 12, I don't realize that this remark stems from her own upbringing and the times in which she grew up. I just feel intimidated, ashamed of the way I feed myself.

I eat like a man, and sometimes I feel like one. When I was in elementary school, I was regularly called a tomboy. I've never been comfortable with that remark. At summer camp, a classmate told me he didn't believe I was a girl. My 5th teacher put me in the boys' group for the end-of-year choir, because my voice was too deep. A friend's mom gave me a large T-shirt, telling me that this was the cut for me, as I had the build of a young man. When I competed in judo, my weight was close to that of boys slightly older than me. So I had to fight against them and very often lost.

This lack of femininity in me questions and complexes me, to such an extent that I don't feel legitimate wearing a dress, and I dread, later on, not looking like a woman.

I turn my gaze to the TV—which is sometimes on in the dining room as the 8 p.m. news approaches. A sublime young woman appears on screen, being interviewed on a set. She's tall and slender. I marvel at her red-rimmed lips, her luminous dark eyes and her beautifully coiffed hair. She's wearing a long, satiny black dress that hugs the curves of her legs. She's so beautiful and exudes such femininity.

I'd love to be like her when I grow up.

I wolf down my last piece of bread and promise myself I'll eat less tomorrow.

The next morning, I step on the scales in my grandparents' bathroom: 56 kg. Horrible. I run away from the reflection of my body in the mirror and put on a pair of basketball shorts.

I can't wait to get back to the South, as there's no Internet connection at my grandparents' house.

A friend of mine, Elsa, whom I met in my first year of college, is always asking me to keep her company by message or webcam. She sometimes writes me very long texts, in which she threatens to call in her big sister if I don't comply with what she tells me to do. In this way, she's kept me away from my school friends and from Chloé D.—a great friend I'd made in 6th, and with whom I laughed a lot.

I felt better before I had Facebook, free of any social obligations when I got out of school. The mere idea of having a cell phone, a portable object on which people can reach me at any time, terrifies me.

The computer is already a source of stress for me. There are two at my parents' house, which we share and are allowed a limited amount of time per person per day. They're in the middle of the living room and are fixed computers. Sometimes, Elsa asks for me while my father is working on them, and I have to negotiate to answer her. I'm afraid of her. Her company is unpleasant, but I can't shake off our relationship.

*

The eve of my return to 5th. I've been back in the south of France for almost a week. The last selection course is over. I check my mailbox every day, hoping to receive the results of the official team. I chat regularly with a girl I met at the last training camp. She's very nice and we get on well. I hope we'll be in the final team together.

Since I've been back home, I've discovered a passion for skipping rope, and I train every day relentlessly to improve my records. I also weigh myself very regularly. I dream of honing my body and feeling better about myself. I'm obsessed with the idea of regaining the figure I had in previous years.

Yesterday, my father complimented a photo of me playing basketball about a year ago: "You were pretty in that photo, you were all finicky!"

I'd love him to think I'm just as beautiful and slender today. I'd like to make him proud. He sometimes shows me photos of a colleague of his training with his daughter for a marathon. This girl is very slim and muscular, and her perfectly defined abs catch my attention every time.

For the past two years or so, I've been training to run with my father on Sunday mornings. These are moments of complicity, when we listen to music together on the way in the car.

We laugh a lot. Before each session, we drink a last sip of water that we call "the victory sip". He's constantly encouraging me and helping me to improve enormously in this discipline. The place where we run is magnificent, a lake bordered by groves. The changing colors of the leaves, grass and surrounding fields punctuate our year as the seasons go by. I love feeling my breath and the strength in my thighs improve with each session. But the effort is sometimes difficult for me when I've had a basketball match the day before, or when the week's training sessions have been intense.

I was disgusted once when my little brother joined us and lost me, even though he'd only trained to run with us twice in the year.

It's because I'm fat.

I turn on the family computer and log on to Facebook. My friend from the selections sent me a message:

"Too bad... you didn't make the final 15. I'm so sorry..."

My heart pounds against my chest, my fingers go numb, my breathing quickens. I can't reach the keys on the keyboard. I reply:

"Really? How do you know?"

She encloses a photo of a table listing the first names of the fifteen girls selected. I scan the table several times with my eyes. My name isn't there. I go straight to my mailbox. I get nothing. I hadn't been notified by the selection coaches. Not a single summary message. Not a single word of encouragement.

A tear rolls down my cheek. I'll have to tell my parents. I'm afraid I'll disappoint them.

I look for them all over the house. They're outside, in the garden.

"I… I didn't get in."

I lower my head, a sob escaping me. My parents smile tenderly at me.

"It's okay, you did your best."

They take me in their arms.

*

Back to school. I take the school bus for the first time with my little brother, who's starting secondary school. We have fun on the way. I hope he likes his new school, that the change doesn't upset him too much and that he makes friends.

Elsa isn't in my class this year. I'm glad. This will allow me to keep my distance from her. On the other hand, I'm glad to hear that Laura is with me.

Laura is a sweet, intelligent girl who went to school with me until CE2[1]. She had to leave our village due to personal problems, so I'm delighted to have her back.

My main teacher is Mrs. Stein. I really like her , she's an extremely funny woman. Her lessons are like theater pieces.

I'm not worried about the prospect of a new school year. I've never really had any problems at school, largely because my parents have always helped me with my homework and lessons. For a long time, my father was a teacher in difficult

1. Children are in CE2 at the age of 8-9.

secondary schools. For the past few months, he has been a prison teacher. His experience and advice have enabled me to progress from year to year. My mother is a graphic designer in a publishing house. She's Basque (on the Spanish side), and learned to speak French when she met my father. Despite the fact that French is not her mother tongue, she supports me in learning every subject.

In this way, my parents have enabled my brothers and me to do well at school. In this area too, I don't want to disappoint them. They don't put too much pressure on us when it comes to school results, but deep down I know they'd be worried if my grades dropped. So I work very assiduously.

I also impose this rigor on myself, as my goal is to enter a general high school in the neighboring town, which has a renowned art option in the region. Drawing is my favorite subject, before sports, photography and writing—other activities I enjoy. When I was younger, I used to spend my nights writing and illustrating stories late into the night. I often woke up with pencils, tubes of glue and scissors spread out on my comforter.

Teachers are sometimes taken aback when I tell them I'd like to go to art school after high school.

"In view of your academic results, you could apply to more serious universities."

I understand their point of view, but I'm not interested in that prospect. I'll work hard to make drawing my profession.

My mother went to art school in Bilbao when she was younger. I've always admired her level of drawing and painting. When I was little, I loved to climb the stairs in our house that led to her studio. I watched each canvas carefully, some in soft, pastel colors, others darker and more eerie, but I loved them all the same. My mother's studio is tucked away in the attic of the house, where damaged tiles let in rays of light and the occasional glint of rain. It smells of oil paint and turpentine. It's a magical, mysterious place.

*

I'm currently reflecting on how much thinner I was at the end of elementary school, when my dermatologist advised me to follow a lactose-free diet to deal with my skin problems. This meant cutting out all foods containing milk, cream and butter—such as cooked bis , yoghurts, cheese and buns. I was even surprised to learn that some brands of industrial ham contained them. I bring up the subject with my parents, claiming that my skin problems are returning. They finally agreed, without being completely convinced.

I'm back on my milk-free diet. I hope it will pay off, and that I'll feel better about myself in time.

As the days go by, I feel that it is becoming less and less difficult for me to avoid lactose-free foods. I am juggling my social and school life, my basketball training and games, and my new diet perfectly. I'm stepping up my jump rope sessions and continuing to run every Sunday with my dad. I feel like I'm making a lot of progress in my running right now, especially during the "final sprint"—the last hundred meters after the last bench on the lake loop. My legs just keep going, even uphill. I'm finally able to keep up with my dad.

I'm hopeful about an upcoming event: the Cross of colleges[2]—a race in two distinct levels (6th/5th and 4th/3th), girls and boys separated. I won it last year, just ahead of two very thin girls whom I had followed throughout the race, then overtaken at the last moment, during the final sprint on the rugby field. My big brother was in the stadium grandstand with all the other schoolchildren, and I was happy and proud to win ahead of him.

It's going to be close this year too, with one or two very athletic girls who are going to give me a hard time.

*

Cross of the 2012-2013 school year. A bang announces the start. Off we go. There are around sixty of us girls. Everyone pushes each other and gives it their all for the first few meters, then the group disperses. I find myself in the lead with two other girls, with stunted, muscular calves, running ahead of me. The sight of their slender, bouncing legs sends a surge of rage through me. I concentrate on my breathing, as my father taught me, and gradually outrun them, right from the first lap of the race. In the middle of the course, as I stride across the schoolyard, I'm alone and bump into my sports teacher, who gives me a high-five. At the finish line, in the rugby stadium, my head teacher, Mrs. Stein, congratulates me and puts a medal around my neck. I'm over the moon and extremely happy.

2. In France, the college is for students aged 11 to 15.

After the race, the school organizes a little tea party. I head there with my friend Laura. Donuts and compotes to drink are laid out on a plastic table. I hesitate for a moment between the two. The sight of the soft, shiny dough of the doughnuts calls me tenderly, but I pull myself together and take only the compote. There's lactose in the doughnut batter.

"You only take this?" asks Laura.

I explain my skin problems, then we sit down in the playground to remake the world.

Winning this race enabled me to qualify for the Cross départemental. I went there with my father on a rainy day. When the race starts, I'm overtaken by countless girls, each more athletic than the last. I lose my footing. I'm not going to make it.

Forty-first. A failure. On the way back, my thighs and face are covered in mud. My father reassures me:

"You did your best."

I'm ashamed of myself.

The Voice

October to December 2012, age 12

3 kg lighter. I feel immense satisfaction, my plan is working perfectly.

Today, I decided to redecorate my bedroom. I detached the photos of fashion and basketball magazines and put them on the wall opposite my bed. It forms a huge mosaic, which I find aesthetically pleasing. All these gorgeous models stare in my direction. One in particular catches my eye. It's a photo of a woman, topless, in black and white, her hair plastered, her face hidden by the shadow of her hat, and her torso tilted slightly back. Her arms are thin and her stomach completely flat. I position myself in the same way as her, facing the narrow mirror in my bedroom. There's a bulge at the bottom of my belly and my arms are chubbier than hers. I'll have to work on that. I promise myself I'll start an abs program tomorrow night. This new resolution obsesses me all day tomorrow.

Every Wednesday afternoon, I have basketball practice. For some time now, my parents have been carpooling with the parents of a girl on my team. She's a skinny teammate, but she doesn't play basketball very well. In the car once, she said to me:

"Look how your thighs shake and touch when the car moves!"

I hate her. I liked it better when my dad took me to training alone.

During basketball games on Saturdays, I'm tough—and sometimes mean—to some of the girls on my team. My position is that of point guard. This role requires precise analysis of the game, knowing the strengths of your teammates and the weaknesses of your opponents. I feel under constant pressure, and I have to be irreproachable to lead us to victory. When I make an ideal pass to a girl on my team and she drops the ball with her hands, it annoys me. One of my coaches, Pascal, puts pressure on me at every time-out—when we're losing—to save the day. Being a leader can be a difficult job. If I lose, I feel a lot of guilt.

I often ask my family not to come and see me at my games. They've never commented on my level of play. They've always been encouraging and supportive, but the fear of disappointing them or making a fool of myself in front of them gnaws at me constantly.

My sporting performance improves as my weight drops. 51 kg. Down 5 kg on the scales since I started my dairy-free diet. I love watching my figure slim down. I think I'm prettier and the feeling of being in control of my diet makes me feel much better.

I refine my clothing style and sometimes allow myself a few feminine touches. I style my hair in a high bun, wear purple cuffed boots and an orange wool scarf. The other day, I tried on a pair of tight pants and a black dress—clothes I wouldn't allow myself to wear before. My mom also gave me matching headbands for a girls' shopping trip.

I love these moments when we both take off in the car to go shopping, on Saturdays when I don't have a match. They're moments of complicity when we talk and laugh a lot. Back then, we'd buy a packet of cookies at the end of our shopping trip and share them together on the way home. Nowadays, I try not to eat cookies outside meals, even if they're lactose-free.

At the end of our last shopping trip together, I found a book called : Le petit livre de la minceur. It's an inventory ranking all the calories per 100 g of raw or processed foods, according to their cooking and brands. I begged my mother to buy it for me.

Since I've had this book, I've learned a lot about nutrition. I've even started keeping a notebook where I record and calculate everything I eat every day. I find this more precise than simply not eating foods containing lactose. I set myself a target of not exceeding 1,300 kcal over the course of the day.

50 kg for 1 m 65. Not bad, but it could be better. I'd like my abs to be more defined and my thighs thinner.

Recently, I've noticed that a voice is increasingly present in my head. It often speaks to me in the imperative, and is increasingly aggressive and judgmental about the people I come into contact with. It sorts things out. I've always had a nasty ca racter, but now it's getting worse and worse. She often contradicts the advice of those closest to me, so I don't know who to believe.

The Voice, which has been with me for a few weeks now, is my new best friend. I confide my doubts to her, *she* helps me achieve my goals and gives me new ones. I trust her, for now.

Now that *she*'s here, I'm gradually plunging into a painful nostalgia. I think back to my early childhood. Truck trips with my family, vacations spent in the Basque country and Normandy, laughter and games shared with my brothers and friends.

I'd like to stay with my loved ones for the rest of my life. The mere idea of moving away from them as an adult to create my own family seems unbearable. I'd like to never leave childhood. They're my family, and nobody else.

Ever since I was a little girl, I've taken a multitude of photos and videos of our daily lives—to make sure I don't forget anything. I spend hours filing these memories away on the family hard drive. The more time passes, the stricter and more meticulous this sorting becomes. Everything has to be perfectly organized. Each video is renamed according to a precise system—locations first and, after a hyphen, a description of the video in a few words. The archives are ordered by month and year, for easy access.

Some days, I immerse myself in these images for hours on end. These moments of contemplation plunge me into a deep melancholy.

*

My mother regularly advises me to go and see Denise, a psychologist who works in an association in my village. Denise is a Quebec-born woman with a unique character. Her hair is very long, gray and slicked back. During our sessions, she looks at me very intently, with bright, compassionate eyes.

"You set the bar too high for yourself in all the activities you practice, you know you're entitled to underperform or fail sometimes?"

*

Repeat this maths exercise until it's perfectly written, without a single cross-out, with each number traced in exactly the same way. I do it. *The Voice* imposes military rigor on my schoolwork and exam preparation. I must be perfect in every way. I must excel.

To make these repetitive exercises more bearable, I sometimes allow myself to do my homework in front of the TV, when my parents aren't at home.

I watch reruns of the first season of *Le meilleur pâtissier*. I love the atmosphere of the bright, colorful tent that serves as the film set. Every piece of music on the show transports me into a fairytale bubble. The garden and château surrounding the tent form an idyllic backdrop, with the camera sometimes following a bird or rabbit enjoying the flowers or the shade of a tree. These scenes remind me of the animated films I grew up with.

My favorite part of the show is the cookies, cakes and pastries prepared by the contestants. Just looking at them makes me feel as if I'm feeding myself.

As time goes by, I'm developing new techniques to help me feel like I'm eating, without putting on weight.

The latest is this: I prepare hearty meals for my family.

One weekend evening, while eating alone with my brothers, I concocted a giant pot overflowing with buttered pasta, covered in cream, grated cheese and slices of salami. I served them this extremely rich dish and prepared myself a pan-fried Asian noodle, accompanied by a few steamed vegetables.

It fascinates and reassures me to see my loved ones gobbling up such high-calorie foods without gaining an ounce. If they don't put on weight with what they eat, nothing can happen to me.

*

I noticed recently that I didn't get my period for the second time. It seems to me that it takes a little time for them to set in at first, but it's still been three months since I've had them. It disgusted me anyway. I'm just afraid the family doctor will ask me about it. We have a visit scheduled with him later on.

I used to hate going to his surgery. We'd go as a family and I'd be forced to weigh myself in front of my nearest and dearest. Since I weighed more than my little brother, I was ashamed of myself.

Today, I go alone with my mother.

Doctor Durand is always kind, positive and welcoming. He's been treating me for several years now and gets on very well with my father—because he's a doctor specializing in sports.

The scales in his office read 48 kg. Dr. Durand is not alarmed by my weight loss.

"It's probably linked to your sporting activities. It's nothing serious! Your build fluctuates a lot at your age."

But I can feel my mother starting to worry. She's been smiling less lately, and her gaze has become sad and distant.

The other day, as we were walking behind the house, I happily announced that I'd fit back into the denim shorts I'd worn at elementary school. She didn't react. Back home, she pulled me aside to talk about something. In her hand was this book: *100 idées pour se sortir d'un trouble alimentaire; anorexie mentale, boulimie, compulsion* (*100 ideas for overcoming an eating disorder; anorexia nervosa, bulimia, compulsion*)...

We were standing at the entrance to the house, I was about to go up the stairs and she said to me, in a serious tone:

"I think you're going through something called anorexia nervosa. It's an illness, but there's help to get through it."

Anorexia? I thought it was just an adjective to describe someone who's very thin. And I'm not skinny. However, the announcement of a potential mental illness seems coherent to me; I can feel that something has changed in me.

One evening, as I was coming out of the bathroom, my father asked me, in a feverish voice:

"Do you make yourself throw up after eating? You can tell me anything, you know..."

I swore I'd never do that. I'd be too afraid of introducing unwanted food into my body and failing to extract it. I sensed that my answer had relieved him a little, but the fear also persisted in his eyes now.

*

The cold is getting to me as winter approaches. I cover myself with many layers of clothing every time I set foot outside. My parents let me set up a space heater in my bedroom at night. I put my pyjamas on it, just before bedtime, while I do my leg and abdominal exercises. The air smells of hot laundry and burnt wool.

Just before falling asleep, I listen to my childhood cartoons to soothe me.

A new bodily change is bothering me a lot at the moment. My toes are purplish, swollen and pale in places. They throb and itch so much at night that they wake me up. My mother asked about it and explained that it must be oedema linked to malnutrition. She massages them with cream sometimes in the evening, to relieve me. I can feel her pain.

46 kg. 10 kg less since I started my lactose-free diet. I finally have slim thighs and a flat stomach. My mirror image is a little less unpleasant. However, there are a few unattractive new features in my reflection. The skin covering my coccyx is blackened with bruises, as I no longer have enough flesh to absorb the friction in this area. In the shower and when I comb my hair, it falls out in fistfuls. My skull is progressively balding: vast holes are forming on my neck and temples,

while my back and arms are covered with a strange fuzz. My mother noticed it the other day and told me it was probably "lanugo"—the fine hair that appears on thin people to replace the layer of fat that normally serves as thermal protection.

These scientific names worry me and make me uncomfortable.

I continue to analyze my reflection. *Your hips are still a little too pronounced.* It's true, *she*'s right.

The Voice is more and more present in my head. *She* orders me to perform certain strange actions sometimes, in return for my thinness. *If you don't slalom between the college pillars before going to class, you'll get fat again. If you don't take three breaks in every meal to reheat it on the stove, you'll get fat again. If you don't turn that light on thirty times, you'll get fat again.* And I'm not even talking about forgetting to exercise or overeat. That would be dramatic, so I'm very vigilant about these things. *She*'d hold it against me for days, even weeks.

She often uses the word: *regrossir*. *She* knows that I'm very afraid of it and that I have to protect myself from it.

*

The days are getting shorter and shorter. Winter sets in. Light disappears and colors fade. I can feel my body's capacity gradually being exhausted. A taste of blood invades my mouth at the end of my running sessions. *The Voice* orders me never to stand still. My knees are constantly knocking together as I sit, covered in bruises.

At the table, every mouthful is a source of anguish as I dissect the contents of my plates and painfully ingest them, crumb by crumb. *The Voice* forbids me to exceed 1,000 kcal per day. Family meals are increasingly silent.

I can't wait for the Christmas vacations, as it's getting harder and harder to keep up with school. Sometimes when I read, words dance and jumble before my eyes. In the corridors of the school, my knees sometimes bend on their own, as if I were about to fall at any moment. My grades haven't dropped, on the contrary, but I have to redouble my efforts to keep up in class and revise at home in the evenings.

My parents and teachers have made sure I'm relieved by setting up a PAI—individualized reception project. Some lessons are replaced by documents that I have to study at home.

Students sometimes make comments about this:

"Don't you have class this afternoon? Too bad."

When I study at home, I bury myself in thick blankets and press myself up against the space heater I take everywhere with me. I revel in the solitude. The silence that reigns in my childhood home reminds me that time passes unstoppably.

*

The Christmas vacations finally begin. I face the stares of family members who haven't seen me since the summer. My Norman grandfather is the only one to compliment me: "You're gorgeous, you look just like your cousins did when they were your age!"

My other relatives watch me discreetly, with tender, concerned eyes. I notice that their attentions are more delicate and cautious than before—as if I'd turned into a porcelain doll.

At Christmas, I asked for a cookbook. I've been peeling through it ever since my parents gave it to me, delighting in every page, contemplating every photograph. Sometimes, I stack up several cookbooks and mount them in my room. I spend hours sneaking a peek. I love talking about these wonderful dishes to my friends and family; I feel as if I'm being nourished by the simple act of describing them orally and talking about them.

One evening, as we were walking outside, I talked a little too much about cooking to my mother, which upset her.

"You can't talk so much about cooking and not eat, I can't take it anymore."

I try to keep these thoughts to myself from now on. Often, before I fall asleep, I imagine that it's the end of the world and I'm alone in a store. I head for the brioches/viennoiseries/buns aisle, and devour everything. These dreams intoxicate and soothe me to sleep.

There's another activity that's been calming me lately: I spend a lot of time drawing pictures of food. I fill entire sheets with meticulous sketches of various dishes. My favorites are pastries and culinary specialties from foreign cultures.

Ever since I was a little girl, I've been fascinated by North Africa and Asia—especially Japan. Their architecture, clothing, customs, cuisine, religions and artistic creations fascinate me. I love writing stories about them, escaping to faraway lands with the characters I invent. I often write and draw during long car journeys or truck trips with my family.

That winter, I was particularly influenced by Michel Ocelot's marvellous universe, and more specifically by his animated film *Azur et Asmar*, which for me contains a fabulous poetry.

*

My Basque grandmother had an operation at the beginning of the Christmas vacations. We went to visit her in hospital with my mother and uncle. My uncle is extremely kind and intelligent. He takes the time to chat with me on the way, and I like the gentle, respectful approach he has with me.

An elderly woman was in my grandmother's room when we arrived, and took advantage of this very appropriate moment to say to me:

"But why have you started a dairy-free diet? You're skinny and you'll stop growing. Look... Asians don't drink milk, that's why they're small."

How could anyone say something so stupid?

*

Back from Christmas vacation. 43 kg. My parents call Dr. Durand for emergency help. He refers us to a clinic that specializes in nutritional problems: the Princess Clinic. I go to the appointment today with my mother, after school.

There are only overweight people waiting at reception. What am I doing here? *They want to turn me into an obese person, that's for sure. It disgusts me. How can it come to this? How can anyone have so little willpower?*

The corridors of the clinic smell of household products, plastic and buttered pasties. The clatter of carts mingles with the steady notes of medical equipment. This is the first time I've been in a clinic like this. The new atmosphere is strangely reassuring. A nurse picks us up and shows us to the door. The first appointment is with a gastroenterologist.

"I advise you to eat fresh cheese triangles in the morning, spread on wholemeal bread."

He chuckles and continues: "I recommend that to my patients, they like it!"

He's crazy. I'd never eat that. Besides, he's a bit fat for a doctor specializing in nutrition, so I won't be taking his advice.

I pretend to listen to him for twenty minutes, then we move on to the next appointment.

A psychologist welcomes me, alone, in his office lit by a yellowish light. The blinds are half-open, and I can see the parking lot outside slowly emptying as night falls.

He's a short man with a greying beard. Discreet glasses sit on the tip of his nose. We chat for a long time. I tell him about my growing fear of eating certain foods. The calorie calculations that obsess me all day. The darkness that consumes me. The voices that haunt me.

After our appointment, the psychologist talks to my mother for a few minutes. I can't hear what they're saying, but the expressions on their faces are serious.

On the way home, I watch the landscape go by, absent. The shadows of the trees dance in the night.

As I do every evening, I perform my physical exercises mechanically, then settle into bed to begin praying. My eyes are closed. I lie on my back, hands clasped. I'm talking to my God.

I grew up in an agnostic family, where we don't practice any religion, so I've invented someone to talk to.

Every night, I repeat the following formula three times: *Please don't make me fat again. Please that my parents are proud of me. Please that I get my period back. Please that my family stays healthy.*

I sometimes add a few nuances depending on the events in my life: *Please let me win tomorrow's match. Please that I pass this or that exam.* I then separate my hands, bring them to my mouth and blow in the direction of heaven, so that my words may be heard.

I never deviate from this ritual.

Once, I fell asleep before performing my "evening prayer", and *The Voice* blamed me all day.

*

Some evenings, I go shopping with my mother. I like to lose myself in the supermarket aisles. I spend hours turning over the items to dissect the nutritional value tables, looking for a miracle food. *This leek soup has fewer calories than this vermicelli soup. Does the same apply to their freeze-dried versions?* These analyses take me hours. My mother is waiting for me at the end of the aisles—her face tense, looking worried. I negotiate to buy foods such as ready-to-use soups, ready-made meals or yoghurts containing sweeteners. Industrial foods make my calculations easier, since the calories they contain are precisely indicated, unlike homemade recipes—whose energy value depends on the cook's goodwill. My mother tries to resist *The Voice,* because she doesn't like chemical foods and "slimming" products. One day, I asked her if we could buy baby food—less calorific than industrial adult meals. Her eyes filled with dismay and despair. She flatly refused:

"No, I can't let you regress that far."

My mother faces *The Voice,* but *She*'s very shrewd and often finds arguments to convince her:

"Better I eat this than nothing..."

As I leave the supermarket, it's very cold. My eyes take in the pitch-black landscape surrounding the dimly lit parking lot. I feel totally empty.

*

The Voice institutes more and more rituals. Every evening before dinner, I stand in the center of the dining room and jump rope. It's the only place in the house where I have room to do it. *200 strokes, not one more or one less. If you don't do them, you won't be allowed to eat.*

No one is to interrupt me during this sequence. *If anyone talks to you or interrupts you to cross the room, you'll have to start all over again.* I hate that. *But it won't hurt to start your set again, you'll burn more calories.* I especially hate being watched, I'd like to be alone with *The Voice.*

My place at the table has changed recently, I'm at the end, between my parents. My brothers are facing each other, a little further away. This new place doesn't make things any easier for me; I can feel my parents watching me.

As it's winter, we eat soup, then a salad. I've worked on a few stratagems over the last few meals to make myself less conspicuous. I take the flattest plate with the smallest indentation. It gives the illusion of being full. *Two ladles, no more.* For the salad, it's less obvious. I arrange two lettuce leaves one on top of the other, then sprinkle a few grains of rice on top—the layering of the salad gives an impression of volume.

My parents scrutinize my plate out of the corner of their eye and start a discussion about future work on the house—phew, they're not worried about the portion I've helped myself to.

"Do you know if we've received any news about the carpenters' estimate?" my mother asks my father.

"No, I haven't."

My father turns to me, glances darkly at my plate and continues:

"In any case, the only estimate we'll get if you go on like this is for your coffin."

A deep silence settles over the room. I leave the table without a sound and head for the stairs, my plate barely started. My father rises abruptly and grabs me by the collar. Then, in a burst of anger and despair, he says to me:

"Are you going to eat your salad?"

He continues, teary-eyed:

"I have to get down on my knees for you to eat, don't I?"

I don't blame him, I understand. Even I can't take it anymore.

Every night, before going to bed, my father comes to my bedside. He takes the time to talk with me, encouraging me, complimenting me, trying to find solutions. Sometimes we talk for hours. We talk about *The Voice*, which we call "the little squirrel".

He tells me to listen to his advice, not that of the little squirrel. I swear I'll get there tomorrow, but deep down I know *The Voice* will be stronger.

The Almond Bar

January 2013, 12 years old

7:05 a.m. Sitting on the edge of my bed, my head rocks gently back and forth. My back is arched. I slide my purple fingers between the grooves of my space heater. I smell something burning. My hands are covered in blisters and purple stains. I drag my body to the clothes I prepared the night before. My feet are increasingly red and swollen, itchy and painful.

Three undershirts, a fleece, a sweater, two tights, a pair of pants, two pairs of socks, a thick scarf.

I'm very cold and get dressed shivering. Before leaving my room, I turn the light on and off six times.

Thumb. Index finger. Thumb. Index finger. Inch. Index finger. Please don't make me fat again.

I go down three flights of stairs, then up again. *If you don't, you'll get fat again.* I finally descend the twenty-one steps to the kitchen. Each step makes a different sound; I know them by heart.

Every morning, I cut an apple into small pieces and meticulously arrange them around my soya yoghurt. *It's prettier that way. It's less scary.* The ritual begins. I prick an apple fragment with the tip of my fork, dip it in a little yoghurt, then let it melt under my tongue. *Above all, don't chew.* All this is done in a clockwise direction, until the fruit rosette fades completely.

60 calories for the apple, 41 calories for the soy yoghurt—it's safer to say 50. The ritual is over after 25 minutes. I wish it could have lasted longer.

As soon as I step outside, the cold pierces my body. My chest, arms and back stiffen. I look out at my childhood garden, where I ran, played and laughed. My little brother walks ahead of me. It's hard to keep up. Each step is harder than the last. *Move forward. Walk faster. Tired.*

At the bus stop, there are other schoolchildren. I can no longer join in their discussions. I try to stand, a few meters away from them, the bag lacerating my shoulders.

The bus finally arrives. A car stops a few meters away. It's my mother. She runs towards me.

"Your bar... You forgot your almond bar..."

She grabs my wrist, slides the bag into the palm of my hand, then takes a step back.

"Try to have a good day."

Her gaze is dark and bright.

Mom, please take me. Please don't leave me alone.

The school hours fly by. I no longer understand anything. I dream of an egg cooking in a casserole full of tomato sauce. The English teacher's words slowly fade.

Recess is the worst part of the day. It's so cold. Laura is by my side. She's the only one who hasn't avoided me since I lost the weight. *Walk. Three laps of the courtyard. And on the last one, hop on the hopscotch, back and forth. Before going to the cafeteria, walk around the manhole three times. If you don't, you'll get fat again.* I do it, as I've done every day for the past few years. Some boys sitting on a bench laugh at me.

I'll never forget those laughs.

I love going into the cafeteria. It's warm and smells good. As we wait in the glass corridor, I imagine what these smells are. I can make out the warm, gourmet scent of roast chicken, spicy notes and the sweet steam of buttered semolina. When I close my eyes, I feel as if these scents are entering my belly. It soothes me. I dream about it. *But this dream is dirty, it would ruin your body and your self-confidence.* Refrigerated desserts don't smell, too bad.

I sit down opposite Laura. To my left, a few girls from our class. Laura plunges her eyes into mine and asks:

"Have you been studying for tomorrow's test?"

"Yes, for a week now. It's stressing me out though, I hope we've already seen the questions in class."

The technique at lunch is to keep the conversation going, to distract attention from my hands, which are gradually hiding the chicken pieces and semolina under paper napkins.

Laura is respectful and discreet, making no remarks. *Everyone is delighted.* At the end of the meal, I grab my tray and struggle to my feet. I walk over to the canteen girls and hand them my napkin-covered plate. At the last moment, I manage to slip in the almond bar my mother brought me at the bus stop this morning. I think of her as I watch the bag fall into the garbage can. It hurts my heart.

Don't even think about it. It's for your own good, 93 calories is a lot for such a small bar. It would have been too much.

The lunch lady gives me a dirty look. *She looks awful.*

On my way out of the cafeteria, I catch a glimpse of Elsa, the girl who bullied me in 6th last year. *Her puppy-dog look makes me feel sorry for her.* I don't feel anything towards that girl anymore, thanks to *The Voice* who protects and guides me. I'm better now that *she*'s talking to me, I feel better in my body. Thinner. More *pure.* Since *She's* been here, other people's voices seem farther away, their lives no longer of interest to me. I don't mind loneliness, *The Voice* keeps me company. I feel liberated from the superfluous, from mediocrity. *The Voice* ranks the people I meet by intellectual interest. If *it* doesn't value you, you don't exist.

*

It's time for gym class. In the locker room, glances are elusive. I change facing the wall, to hide my ribcage. The girls are chattering away. *They talk and laugh so loudly, they're unbearable. Their bodies ooze fat. They disgust me.*

An arduous walk awaits us in the cold and fog, towards the village arena. The gym teacher scrutinizes me for a few yards, then pulls me aside.

"You've lost a lot of weight Oihana... You know... It's important to eat, to refuel. Without gas, the car won't move, you know? The ideal is... Look, I eat in moderation and..."

That's it. Don't listen to him anymore. I can't hear him anymore.

We enter the arena, which doubles as a sports and entertainment venue. It smells of straw and damp. Some of the doors no longer close, letting in an icy wind that blows through my ribs and back. Everyone in my class is running and screaming, *never stopping*. It's like a continuous bellowing. *A herd of animals*. The gym teacher makes us stretch on the floor. Every movement exhausts me. *You can't even do that anymore.*

On the way home from school in the evening, my mother reminds me that we have an important appointment with a new doctor she's met. We get into the car.

The Maison des Adolescents[3]

January 2013, 12 years

Raindrops slap against the windshield. It's dark out. The road seems long, my mother's gaze fixed on the horizon. I'm afraid of what awaits me at this new appointment. My head slips into my thick scarf and I close my eyes. I wish everything would stop.

By the time we reach town, the rain is coming down harder and harder. We decide to take a shortcut through a sunken neighborhood. I can hardly keep up with my mother's pace. I cling to her arm. My knees buckle on the way down, and sometimes give out, as if they've stopped working. My neck muscles are weak, and I lean my head against my mother's shoulder. In this part of town, streetlights are few and far between. Faint lights sway before my wet eyes. We make our

3. The "Maison des Adolescents" is a free and confidential public service in France for young people aged 11 to 25. It offers a welcoming place where adolescents can drop in without an appointment to talk about any concern. Multidisciplinary professionals provide listening, guidance, and orientation to appropriate support services.

way towards a street that climbs towards the meeting place. It's going to be tough. I lower my head, cling tighter to my mother's arm, then we climb together, one step at a time, breathless. Stunned by the winter rain.

We finally pass through the door of La Maison des Adolescents. I'm surprised to find that this place is nothing like a doctor's surgery. It's a rather cozy duplex apartment, with a reception area featuring a colorful sofa and an oval table covered with felt-tip pens and sheets of paper. A staircase rises against the wall to the left of the table—I wonder if the doctors are upstairs. The secretary's desk faces the entrance, at an angle to the waiting room. She smiles tenderly at us.

"Oihana and her mom, right? You can wait on the sofa, Mrs. Roger will be down shortly to fetch you."

Sitting on the sofa, I hear a woman's powerful voice above us, faintly muffled by the ancient floorboards. A few minutes pass, and then a door opens upstairs, releasing the woman's voice to be heard more clearly. Suddenly, heels click against the floor, then race down the stairs.

I see Mrs. Roger for the first time. She's dressed in a long white blouse, her hair brown and bobbed. Thick glasses frame her bright, dark eyes. She invites us to follow her upstairs. We enter her office. She asks my mother a few questions, then gets me on the scale: 42.3 kg.

"Oihana, I'll give you one last chance to show us that you can stabilize those 42 kg."

She points to the falling body mass index curve on my health chart.

"If you drop below 42 kg by our next appointment in two weeks' time, we'll have no choice but to admit you."

I nod shyly in agreement, then Mrs. Roger turns to my mother.

"Until then, we'll have to ban sports."

"Can she continue skipping rope, or is considered a sport?"

"No. We're stopping all forms of hyperactivity. Also forbid her to cook, as well as any contact with cooking shows and books."

Mrs. Roger is impassive. My mother pulls up alongside her. I feel lost and alone. She wants to take everything away from me. *The Voice* disagrees. I sense that Mrs. Roger knows other *Voices*. She knows how it works. She scares the hell out of me.

After the appointment with Mrs. Roger, I meet the psychiatrist at the Maison des Adolescents: Mrs. Leclerc. Her office is on the same floor as Mrs. Roger's. I don't dare tell her.

I don't dare tell her everything I'm feeling, for fear she'll tell Mrs. Roger, since they work together.

*

When I come home in the evening, my mother makes sure I don't go skipping. *The Voice* gets indignant and screams so loud in my head that I curl up on the floor and press my hands hard against my ears. *You'll get fat again! That's for sure! All our efforts will be wasted and your complexes will return.*

So I make up for it by doubling the series of exercises I do in my bedroom. I work out in front of the mirror, my legs rising one after the other. Machinically, with what little energy I have left—like an articulated puppet. I float totally in my basketball team tee-shirt. My eyes are blank and circled in black, I no longer recognize myself.

For the last time, I position myself in the same way as the magazine mannequin that decorates my wall. Bust slightly bent backwards. That's it, I've got the same belly and the same arms as her—if not even skinnier. *You've done it.*

*

The next day at school, I confide in my friend Laura at length. My throat tightens, the words are hard to get out. Suddenly, I burst into tears. She takes me in her arms. I'm not usually very tactile, but I let her. It's nice, I needed it.

Today, we have an exam on classical music called: *Dans les Steppes de L'Asie centrale*. We have to answer several questions while the teacher plays the music in the background. I studied so much the day before that I cried with fatigue. I couldn't understand everything. My mom advised me to close my eyes if it was too difficult on exam day, to enjoy the moment and what the music evoked in me. I follow her advice and let myself be guided towards a fabulous dream, on the edge of an infinite desert. A group of Tuaregs dressed in blue tunics walk in the distance, accompanied by a camel. A palm tree silhouetted against the starry night.

I open my eyes, find the strength to answer all the questions, then turn the page to draw the scene from my dream.

The music teacher walks past me, smiles fondly and whispers, “Nice drawing”.

*

I don’t know how I’m going to keep the 42 kg weight down. I feel as if I’ve lost control of everything and am losing weight like crazy, without being able to do anything about it. I hide under layers of loose clothing, because the thinness of my body is now too visible. When my father takes me in his arms and feels my shoulder blades under his hands, he says:

“You look like you’ve got angel wings”.

The situation is starting to scare me. My parents do their best to persuade me to eat, but I refuse any suggestion. *They won’t put a spoon in your mouth anyway. It’s up to you.* I’d like to stop falling. I’m fine with this weight. *If you increase the amount you eat, you won’t maintain your weight, you’ll get fatter and feel worse about yourself. Just like before.*

She’s right.

In the evening, when I sit down to dinner, I try to make a few efforts. I reluctantly eat a slice of wholemeal bread. My parents rejoice at every little advance, their eyes filling with pride. Making them proud is what I’ve been trying to do for so long. I love seeing them like this. But *The Voice* grabs my hand and pulls me close, hard.

It lures me into a completely dark place, where there are no bodies, no problems and no noise. Darkness develops my sense of poetry and my creative faculties. In leanness and exhaustion, I discover the quintessence of art and soul. *Purity.*

*

The psychologist at my village association, Denise, recommended that my mother prepare a bath infused with lavender essences.

I thought I saw death dancing above me that day, through the hot steam of the scented bath. She promised that my pain would cease if I joined her.

This presence left me when my mother came into the room to weigh me.

39.1 kg.

The next day, we had an appointment at the Maison des Adolescents.

“Do you know what Oihana means?”

Mrs. Roger looks into my eyes, her expression completely neutral. She continues:

“We’re going to have to admit you.”

Pediatrics

February 2013, Age 12

Pediatric hospital emergency room parking lot. February 23, 2013, 2:15 p.m. It's snowing. I clasp my icy hands to my parents' coats. The three of us walk together towards a large sliding glass door. The emergency room is packed with children of all ages. What am I doing here? I'm not sick. I feel guilty at the sight of a young boy with a hearing aid in front of me.

A nurse moves quickly, around the four corners of the waiting room, then approaches us.

"Follow me."

She guides us into a small, white-walled room cluttered with medical equipment. Members of the nursing staff join her. Everyone busies themselves around me. A nurse sticks electrodes on my arms and torso, while one of her colleagues takes my temperature and blood pressure. Then they measure me. Then they weigh me. 38.4 kg. Down 18 kg in 6 months.

An orderly dictates a multitude of data, which her colleague transcribes onto sheets of paper. Bradycardia,

41 bpm. Hypothermia. Alopecia. Marked asthenia. Thyroid insufficiency. Suddenly, a sturdy woman lifts me into a wheelchair. I let her. Not a word leaves my mouth. My muscles and thoughts no longer resist.

The nurse pushes me through the hospital corridors. My neck no longer holds my head, it falls slightly to one side. I used to love running, dancing, walking on the beach and in the mountains, but now I can't even stand up. My parents are there, walking briskly beside the wheelchair.

We arrive at a room. No. 30.

The nurse leaves us alone in the room. I rush straight to the radiator and press myself against it, a blanket draped over my shoulders. My hands are burning. I close my eyes.

A group of adults in white coats enter the room. Within seconds, they surround the bed I'm sitting in, then turn to my parents. One of them quickly explains what's coming next. Infusion. Blood test. Anxiolytics.

"We'll start nasogastric tube feeding tomorrow."

I don't understand much... The entire medical team leaves the room in an orderly ballet, except for one nurse who pricks my forearm. I'm connected by a tube to a machine that flashes and beeps at regular intervals. It looks like a robot.

My parents stay with me for a good two hours, then have to go home to look after my two brothers. They hug me, then leave the room. Goodbyes are painful. When I'm alone again, I sink into the hospital bed, my hands plunged into the pockets of my tracksuit. My faithful doudou, Canou, keeps me company. My parents gave him to me when I was 8. I place him on either side of my neck, then drift off to sleep, lulled by the sound of medical equipment.

I've always dreamed of having a pet. When I was little, I used to look out of my bedroom window at the garden and imagine running and playing with a dog for hours on end.

Last night, on my last night at home, my parents announced that we'd be adopting a dog when I got out of hospital. I'm thrilled. To tide us over, my father decorated the inside door of my hospital room with a Jack Russell sticker. We look at it together and laugh, imagining our future adventures. We call him "Jackie".

"When Jackie's here, all this history will be a distant memory."

The walls of my hospital room are decorated with a mural. It faces my bed, and I spend hours looking at it. Two riders on royal blue horses gallop towards immense golden dunes. The sky is dotted with orange clouds, like gold dust.

A small television stands above the painting. The bedroom window overlooks the pediatric ward's inner courtyard, in which there is a small children's playground. I get up twice a day to observe this patch of greenery framed by gray facades. There are never any children playing there.

"We're going to put in your catheter, Oihana."

A nurse and an orderly stand at the foot of my bed. My mother came to visit me this morning, and she's sitting next to me. I don't know what to expect. The nurses count to three, then slide a long tube into my nostril. The sensation is very unpleasant. I feel as if they're piercing something in my nose. A tear rolls down my cheek. The probe advances millimeter by millimeter, rasping the mucous membrane of my nostril. Suddenly, my breathing stops. The probe reaches my throat, then I feel it slowly descend to the inside of my stomach. I struggle to swallow and breathe throughout the whole operation.

"That's it, it's over."

A plastic-tasting foreign object has entered my body.

"We'll turn on the nutrition pump tonight, at the beginning of the night."

As soon as the nurses leave, I rush for the feeding bag. *1,500* kcal THE bag! That's a lot. What am I going to do? I share my fears with my mother, who tries to reassure me:

"It's for your own good. You'll be fine!"

But it's no use. 1,500 kcal is 500 kcal more than I've been eating for two months. What's more, I won't be able to compensate with physical activity. There's a porthole on my bedroom door. I'm not even allowed to walk in the corridors, in the courtyard or in my room. They consider this hyperactivity.

During the day, the hospital staff serves me three meal trays. *You can't eat more calories than they're going to put through your tube tonight in your sleep! That's force-feeding. Because of them, you won't be able to enjoy your weight regain by tasting the foods you crave. They'll make you fatter and all your efforts will be wasted.*

In that case, I'll restrict myself even more than when I was at home. To counter the probe. It's going to be difficult, I'm constantly thinking about food, day and night.

For three days, I return each tray as soon as it's begun. I scatter the rice and Vichy carrots around, pretending I've "tried" to eat. It doesn't work with the medical team. They understand everything.

The nurses on the morning round told me that a doctor would be visiting me in the early afternoon. After returning my lunch tray, I fall asleep, my head resting against my Canou blanket. Suddenly, someone knocks on the door and enters my room. It's Mrs. Roger. Her presence terrifies me as much as it reassures me. I knew she worked simultaneously at the Maison des Adolescents and the pediatric hospital, but I didn't think she'd follow me here.

Ms. Roger asks me about the start of the hospitalization, and then explains the rest of the treatment.

"The aim is to stabilize your weight at first, Oihana. Then gradually work your way up to 48 kg... which would be a suitable discharge weight. We'll take it one step at a time."

A few hours later, she tells my parents that my weight has dropped again since I went into hospital. 400 g less, or exactly 38 kg.

I still have to gain 10 kg to get out of here. All my work will be destroyed. I'm afraid I'll go back to suffering. And I won't be able to stop if I start gaining weight again.

*

My parents told me that my big brother, Peio, would be visiting me today. Peio is three years older than me. When I was little, he was an example to me. I wanted to be like him.

Unfortunately, exchanges with my brothers have become increasingly rare of late. It's very difficult for me to explain to them the reasons for my self-destruction. I find it hard to understand myself.

My parents enter my room first, then Peio appears. He takes three steps, observes my surroundings, hands shoved into his coat pockets, then says:

"You're fine here, it's a big room!"

There's a silence. Then Peio starts to cry. His eyes are red, and he smiles tenderly as he looks at me. Then he walks over to me.

"You're going to make it. We're all with you, we believe in you."

My father takes a photo of us. I'm bedridden, a probe in my nose, my skull protruding, fine wrinkles around my mouth that sketch a smile, the little hair I have left gathered in a bun. Peio stands beside me, leaning slightly, a protective hand on my shoulder, his eyes red with tears. We both look at my father.

The next day, my little brother, Unai, also visits me with our parents. Unai is quieter than Peio. He sits in an armchair at the back of the room. I'd like to reassure him that everything's going to be all right, that I'll be joining him at school soon, and that everything will be as it was before. But no words come out of my mouth. I can hardly get my back out of bed. The drugs I'm given slow me down.

The sorrow felt by the relatives who visit me at makes me realize that the situation is serious and difficult to bear. I'm touched by every gesture and attention they give me. But it's hard for me to interact with them, because I'm so tired all the time and have so few emotions.

I let myself be carried along by the millimetric daily routine of the hospital.

*

Every morning, the orderlies come to fetch me when the communal shower becomes available. It's the only time of day when I take a few steps. I leave my room, turn right into the corridor, then turn on the handle of the shower room. It's a small room covered with beige tiles on the floor, ceiling and walls. There's something hypnotic about the repetition of these squares. As soon as I turn on the shower, the room fills with a dense steam that veils the grid around me.

Today is a hair-washing day. My mom is coming to visit me later, to do my hair. I lean my head back to wet the top of my head, then forward to wet the back of my neck. Warm water drips down my temples and forehead, then coats my face. Still leaning forward, I feel something slide down my throat and nostrils, then out of my nose.

The nasogastric tube hits the shower tiles beside my feet. It's completely out of my body, on the floor, surrounded by blood that's thinning in the water.

My gaze remains locked on this scene for a few seconds, then, all at once, my head empties. A weight falls on my back, my legs give way. I collapse to the ground. My head hits the floor.

It's dark, I can't see a thing. I hear distant moaning—probably from a child.

But who's making all that noise?

The more time passes, the more these moans seem to belong to me.

I open my eyes with difficulty. I'm naked on the floor, crying, sprawled against the tiles of the hospital shower. The catheter is next to my head. Hair is all over the floor.

I try to get on my knees and find the door handle. Then I limp across the corridor to my room. The ward is very quiet, and I don't pass a single carer.

Once I've reached door No. 30, I crawl in and grab a pair of panties, then lie down in bed. I press the nurse call button.

Before long, I'm surrounded by nurses performing reactivity tests. My mother enters the room.

It was the first time I'd ever felt unwell.

The nurses left the room when my condition stabi lise. Then my mother begins to comb my hair, which continues to fall in handfuls. She carefully deposits it in the dustbin in my room, without making a sound.

*

The days repeat themselves in the same setting, where I can no longer discern the passage of time. My mother visits me at lunchtime, my father in the evening when he gets off work. At the moment, he's learning at the prison where he teaches that it's important for prisoners to take the time, several times a day, to gaze at a distant point—if they can. This gesture is necessary to preserve visual acuity and prevent the eyes from becoming accustomed to proximity. So I spend several minutes a day observing the deserted playpen in the middle of the pediatric ward's inner courtyard.

The nurses forbid the presence of my parents during mealtimes. So my father comes to visit me every day before dinner, between 5.30 and 6.45 p.m. Then from 7.45 p.m. to 9 p.m., after the meal. In between, he goes for walks in the forest, looking forward to hearing the cuckoos sing, heralding the arrival of spring. I'd like to be with him on these walks, but I'm still not allowed out.

To pass the time, I watch *Un dîner presque parfait*. The medical team forbids me to watch cooking shows. So, as soon as a nurse enters my room, I change the channel.

After dinner, my father joins me. We talk for over an hour; time flies when he's around. Then, just before he leaves my room, we blow on each other's hands so that a kiss flies to the other. Then we spread our arms. I watch his fingers disappear behind my bedroom door until the last second.

*

Mrs. Leclerc, a psychiatrist at the Maison des Adolescents, visits me once a week. It's hard for me to describe my emotions to her, because I feel so tired. Her presence is strangely reassuring, reminding me of life outside the hospital.

I'm gradually getting to know the nursing staff, the day and night shifts.

I really like Jennyfer. A young nurse who is very gentle with me, and whose pretty face is highlighted by locks of blond hair. When it's evening and the ward is quiet, she sits beside my bed to keep me company. I ask her questions about her life outside the home. She tells me about evenings out with her friends, her budding love affair with a young man, the jogging she does around town.

Jennyfer sometimes strokes my forehead and says:

"All this will come for you too one day, I'm sure of it."

There's Jonathan, too, an orderly who used to play basketball when he was my age. He speaks very kindly to me, and is interested in my sporting past. When I go to shower in the morning, he puts my Canou cuddly toy back on top of my bed, head up.

On the other hand, there are women on the medical team whom I detest, who suspect me of making myself vomit, throwing food down the toilet or being hyperactive in my room. The mistrust is constant, to the point where the bathroom door to my room is locked all day. I have to press the nurse's bell to get to the bathroom. During the day, when the ward is crowded, the wait can last for long minutes. Sometimes I'm afraid I won't be able to hold it in any longer.

One day, I asked the orderly passing by my room:

"Why can't the bathroom door stay open? It would be simpler."

"If you're allowed access to the toilet, you'll make yourself vomit or throw food... You anorexics are all liars anyway. I'm used to it by now!"

No matter how much I swear to them that I've never made myself vomit, they don't believe me. They don't believe me.

One of the nurses is sometimes brusque in the care she gives me. I get anxious when she has to change my catheter. She nags and nags, changing the nostril tube several times—as if she can't get it through. The pain is so intense that I cry.

A young girl once put the tube in my mouth and made me drink a glass of water, but the procedure was quick and painless.

*

I've been at the paediatric hospital for three weeks now. Mrs. Roger grants me my first leave, a three-hour outing with my parents. I put on my shoes for the first time in a while, and cling to my parents' arms. We wander through the corridors of the pediatric ward, then make our way to the exit. It's a labyrinth; I don't think I've ever known us to walk so far to get to my room. The large sliding glass door opens in front of us. The light dazzles me. I feel the air caress my skin. The smells and sounds of the city seem altered, amplified. The hustle and bustle of the people in the parking lot stuns me, and I can't keep my eyes on them.

We go for a walk in the forest with my parents, and I use a stick I find on the ground to help me stand.

*

The Voice has lost a little control over my life since I've been hospitalized. Mrs. Roger doesn't leave any room for *her* to express herself. She locks us both in separate rooms, but we sometimes get together when the meal trays are served.

Remember that you'll have 1,500 kcal going through the tube tonight. You don't do any physical activity during the day, so don't tell me you need extra food?

To congratulate myself on not having touched the meal trays, *she* tells me exotic, scintillating stories. *Pure* stories where the characters are delicate and devoid of vice. Sometimes *she* helps me draw by putting her hand on mine, because my fingers can no longer hold the markers my mother gave me. I no longer have the strength or the desire to create, but *She* thinks that drawing is an important practice, that I'll do something with it later, that I need to increase my discipline in this area. When I fall asleep, *She* quietly returns to her room.

A month in hospital.

"40 kg. The weight is coming on very slowly, so you'll have to try and put some weight on it or we'll increase the nutrition bags."

The more the weeks go by, the more the feeling of loneliness weighs on me. I feel imprisoned, under constant surveillance. The constant medical presence and lack of privacy affect me.

The other day, the orderly who woke me up found a puddle of liquid food in my bed, next to my shoulder. The tube of the nasogastric tube had become slightly unscrewed during the night. I immediately realized that I wouldn't be believed if I said I had nothing to do with it. I tried to defend myself, but to no avail. The medical team took away my leave. My parents tried to negotiate, but the doctor replacing Mrs. Roger was intransigent.

I'm at least a little comforted by the idea of having lost a few calories in the process. *It's a blessing in disguise.*

Before arriving at the hospital, I had the impression of seeing the volume of my organs under the dry skin of my belly. I found it beautiful and reassuring. There wasn't an ounce of fat left on my body. *The Voice* congratulated me and left me alone for a while. Now, the skin on my belly is less nervous, smoothing out gently. It's very unpleasant to see this part of my body change. *You're getting fatter. You make no effort to face them.* To calm *The Voice,* I do a few sheathing exercises in my bed, discreetly, when no one is watching me behind the window of my bedroom door.

Tonight, when my father paid me a visit, I felt the irresistible urge to go home with him, to return to my childhood bedroom, to everyday life in my little village.

"We still have a little way to go, but we'll get there soon, I swear. We'll be fine."

I can't stand being forced to lie in bed all day, spied on by the nurses, force-fed by the tube. I get up from my bed in one swift movement, then gather my things in a bag, screaming. I rip off the dog's wall sticker and take him with us.

"I've had enough! I can't take it anymore... I want out! I want out now. Get me out of here, I want to live outside..."

I cry. I scream. I throw my bag on the floor, kick the bed, clutch my hands tightly to my head. My father stays by my side, trying to calm me down. Then an orderly enters the room.

"Let's calm down. Oihana, sit back down. Until the doctors give the go-ahead for your discharge, there's nothing we can do anyway."

Sad. Exhausted. I sink into bed as my father and the orderly leave the room. I stare at the gray ceiling tiles, plunged into darkness. I count them, in different ways. Diagonally, vertically. Each time, I get lost along the way, then start again.

*

The days are long, because I can no longer work, read or draw.

"Your brain is malnourished, Oihana. If you want to resume your passions, you're going to have to fight and be patient," Mrs. Roger tells me.

I sometimes wonder what will happen when I go back to school. How am I going to make up for all those missed classes?

My mother brought me a surprise yesterday. Everyone in my class wrote me a note of encouragement. Everyone wrote it down on a piece of paper. 27 messages of encouragement in all. Here are a few from my personal archives:

> *It's Axel, I wish you good luck, Oihana (because you need it). I send you lots of kisses. Take care, we're with you!* Axel L.

I support you and I think all the 5e2 care about your health. Without you, the class wouldn't be the same. Come back soon! Sylvain B.

Good luck, Oihana, I hope you get out of this hellhole soon. I miss you so much! Lucas T.

Hello, Oihana, the 5e2 told me about your illness. Listen, you're a fighter. Fight to the end, try to overcome the illness, don't be afraid of what happens next. Even if you're a bit scared, don't think about it. We're all rooting for you, so hang in there. Give it your all (but not too much). We all love you! Jordan L.

I hope you're doing well where you are. I miss you in Latin, Techno and SVT club. I've missed you a lot since you left. Orienteering with Marie is different than with you, I really miss you! But don't worry about me, I'm fine. Big kisses! All the best. Laura D.

It's hard for me to react to so much love and support. I'm no longer aware of who I am or what I'm going through. I'm trying to write a letter of thanks to my whole class, but the words are all jumbled up in my head. I can no longer form sentences.

The next morning, as I get out of the shower, I decide to do my own hair. I look at my reflection in the toilet mirror in my bedroom. My eyes follow the probe that pulls at my nostril and wraps itself around my bun during the day when I'm not plugged in, blocked by a barrette—a technique I've put in place so that it doesn't catch on the objects around me. Some of the nurses congratulate me on this method, smiling:

"Clever! I've never seen that before."

I get used to the plastic taste of the wire going down my throat, and to my changing features. My face is slightly less sunken, and tape is placed over my nose and cheek to stabilize the probe. My eyes, on the other hand, are still foreign to me. I run the brush through my fraying hair and look at my eyes set deep into my skull. As translucent as glass, empty, without a sparkle.

My head is suddenly drained of blood. My legs give way and my temples hit the ground hard.

Everything goes black. The same childish moans as last time.

I wake up sprawled out on the floor, then crawl across it again, to the call bell for the carers.

Mrs. Roger comes to see me. I tell her I need to get out of the hospital.

"Oihana... the outside is a hostile environment for you at the moment... Like some kind of jungle. Our job is going to be to give you the strength you need so that you can fend for yourself later, without our help."

*

Two months passed in the hospital. Winter gradually gave way to spring. The little tree in the pediatric courtyard finally turns green. My father tells me that the cuckoos, which signal the arrival of fine weather, are finally here.

"I can hear them. But when I get closer, little by little, to catch a glimpse of them… Nothing! They stop singing."

I now weigh 40.9 kg. It's not going fast enough for the medical team. My parents and Mrs. Roger discuss a transfer to a psychiatric hospital specializing in eating disorders. I'm delighted by the idea. I can't stand being surrounded by carers who don't understand anorexia, who criticize it as if it were a whim, a choice. As if I'd rather be in enclosed within four walls than out with my friends, laughing and playing.

The psychiatric hospital to which I'll be sent is in Bordeaux—a 2.5-hour drive from my parents' house. An ambulance will pick me up tomorrow, so that my parents and I can visit it.

I won't have time to say goodbye to Jennyfer, the nurse I loved so much.

The Psychiatric Hospital

May 2013, age 13

The ambulance drops us off in the parking lot of the psychiatric hospital. It's an off-white building, pierced by rows of tiny windows. We climb the stairs to the third floor, where the 8-14-year-old unit is located.

A woman opens the door, and invites us to follow her to visit the floor. We're in the middle of a long corridor, which runs in two opposite directions. At the far left is a translucent window whose light dazzles me. The corridor is punctuated by ten rooms whose doors are open. Our first step is to the right, where we discover the communal living area. Three young children are sitting on an orange sofa. They don't move much, chatting in silence. A bookcase divides the space into two distinct sections. Picture windows diffuse pale rays of light from the back of the room.

Suddenly, the distant melody of a piano reaches me from the other end of the corridor.

The woman showing us around leads us in.

"This is the small music room, where young musical patients can express themselves. Further on, you'll find the communal dining room..."

My gaze freezes on the girl playing the piano. Her hair is fine and black, her skin very pale. She's sitting next to her music teacher. Her bony hands brush the piano keys. She repeats the same passage several times, and stops at the same moment, when the melody speeds up.

Her music teacher gives her a few tips, then whispers:

"You'll get the hang of it, Hélie.

Hélie tilts his head slightly towards us, and I notice a probe coming out of his nose. And so am I.

I see the title of the piece she's playing on the score: *Comptine d'un autre été*, by Yann Tiersen.

*

First day of my transfer to the psychiatric hospital. A nurse directs us to the ward exit door.

"Say goodbye to your parents Oihana, you won't be able to see them again for a week."

A week away from them, in this place where I don't know anyone. It scares the hell out of me. They hug me, then leave the corridor. I press my hand against the window overlooking the staircase, my father puts his on the other side.

The nurse leads me to a place where my belongings are searched. Food, sharp objects, aerosols, medicines, shoelaces and cell phones are forbidden.

First dinner at 6:30 p.m.

"Initially, meals will be served in your room. We'll then assess when you're ready to join the communal dining room."

Fine, I have no desire to eat with the others anyway. An orderly enters my room and places a lunch tray on a small table leaning against a white wall. I place a photo of my parents and brothers facing me. The table is aligned with my bedroom door, which must remain wide open for most of the day.

The quantities are astronomical. The pasta oozes fat and the cauliflower is covered with a thick layer of cheese and white cream. There are TWO slices of ham. They're crazy. I won't touch it.

I'm forced to sit in front of my lunch tray for 45 minutes, even if I don't eat. I stare longingly at the photo of my family, tenderized by each of their faces, then sweep my eyes across the white wall.

Three quarters of an hour later, a fat, bearded nurse collects my tray. I read on the label sewn to his chest that his name is Frédéric, Fred.

"You know, if you want to get out of here, you're going to have to show a little more willpower. The meal trays have to be completely finished before they go to the communal dining room."

"But I'm not hungry because of the probe..."

"It's not my problem. If you don't follow protocol, you'll stay here."

I'm stuck here. Detained. My father, who came to see me after every dinner in pediatrics, isn't here.

I miss him already. I ask Frédéric if I can call my parents.

"No. You can call them in three days."

Three days? My throat tightens. I've never gone a day without them or without having them on the phone.

"I want to talk to my parents. Please... I need to. Let me call them!"

He refuses categorically. Tears roll down my cheeks. I scream and start banging on the walls. Fred closes my bedroom door.

"Let me out!!! I've had enough! Let me..."

After a few minutes of screaming, I collapse on my bed, exhausted. An orderly opens the door.

"Calm down."

She hands me some tissues. I tell her, crying, that I'd like to go home and go on vacation with my family.

"Look at you... You can see that you wouldn't be able to."

While I'm blowing my nose, I hear a nurse's voice echoing in the corridor. He's on the phone.

"Are you Oihana's parents? She's doing very well, don't worry."

I feel powerless, imprisoned.

*

That evening, the nurses take me to the communal living area, where two young children are watching the film *Venus Beauty*, plunged into the dark.

"You have to fit in with the others if you want to be perceived well by the doctors."

I take a seat next to the two children. My knees knock together mechanically, to burn off a few calories before the catheter is plugged in. One of the two nurses standing behind us taps my shoulder:

"Stop!"

I love Audrey Tautou, but this film is a bore. I watch every scene with a sad, distant gaze, my eyes full of tears.

I miss my family terribly.

I'm 13 and alone, locked up in a faraway place with people I don't know.

At night, I curl up in bed to protect myself from the screams of the other children in the unit.

The sounds terrify me.

I wake up at 8 a.m.

The breakfast tray is served to me on the table in my room. I have to choose between two packs of cereals or rusks with butter and jam. I choose the rusks. They're small, but served by the dozen, in two packs of six. *Nobody eats that much in the morning. It's enormous.* But sweet cereals scare me even more.

But I remembered what the nurse told me yesterday. If I don't touch the meal trays, I won't get out of here. So I bite into a rusk with my teeth, and eat it very slowly, facing the white wall of my room. Every crumb is torture.

Shortly afterwards, I meet up with the other children in the common room, then isolate myself with Hélie, the other anorexic on the ward. She looks at me silently as I tell her about my breakfast, then says:

"I'd advise you to choose cereals instead of rusks in the morning... Even if they serve two 30g packs... there are still fewer calories than in the twelve rusks with butter and jam..."

She adds:

"By the way, don't try flushing food down your bedroom toilet. I tried once, and the food came to the surface a quarter of an hour later... A nurse found out."

Hélie is a sweet, caring girl who speaks very slowly. I think she's known about the disease longer than I have. I ask her if she has the same fears and physical pain as I do. If she, too, has a *Voice* in her head. She nods softly to each question I ask, her eyes blank, thinned by the correction of her glasses.

After a short silence, she asks me in turn:

"Are you depressed?"

"No... Well, I don't think so.3

"Normally, yes... All anorexics are depressed. Anorexia is a form of depression. A slow suicide."

*

I manage day after day to eat a little more of the contents of my lunch trays, despite the fear and suffering. *It's horrible, but you do it just to get out of this awful place. Once you're out, you'll lose the extra pounds. I'm not sure you can do it twice in a row.*

The Voice is confined to the same room as me. *She* keeps me company throughout the day. After lunch, the medical team locks us in our rooms for two hours. This is when *The Voice* is at her most talkative. *She* orders me to write down all the calories consumed in a small notebook, which I discreetly hide in my bag so that the nurses don't discover it. *She* lists all the disadvantages of a sedentary lifestyle in terms of body fat gain. Then *She* rehashes the discussions with the nurses, whom *She* hates just as much as I do. I feel less alone.

During "quiet time", I spend long minutes sitting on a chair in front of my bedroom window, watching the parking lot outside. I'd love to be outside, to feel the breeze in the air and the warmth of the sun on my face. The windows here don't open. They're only unlocked during the half-hour of housekeeping when we're forced to stay in the common area. I find it terribly sad.

"It's so that people don't jump out of the window," says Hélie.

I sometimes try to occupy myself by starting books. I took one with me, *The Last Elf*, which I love. I'd love to reread it, but I can't, because *The Voice* speaks too loudly in my head.

So I close my eyes and doze off, trying to forget the place I'm in.

The days are so heavy that I've started keeping a chart, drawn on a sheet of paper with colored markers. Every morning, I tick off the day I'm about to start.

*

Tonight, it's lasagne. *The portion is monstrous, overflowing the plate.* I eat a quarter of it. I chew the dough, swallow the minced meat and the thick sauce. It's difficult. I pull my chair back from the table and start to cry. The nurses clear my tray.

Lasagne's too much. You have to compensate. Just before going to bed, I turn on my bedside lamp and start doing sit-ups, on the floor, with my legs up on my bed. I put a pillow under my back so that my spine doesn't rub against the floor. As I'm connected to the feeding machine, the movements are difficult. I'm afraid of tearing a cable.

I'm in my underwear, with a bra that's far too large, my ribs and arms gaunt. *You have to go up to 100,*" says *The Voice.* I do it. I hadn't done abdominals since I went into hospital. These frenetic movements intoxicate me.

Suddenly, I see the head of an orderly in the doorway to my room.

Oh, no!

"What are you doing? Stop that right now!"

"I don't feel well... I miss my parents. I need to talk to someone... a shrink."

"We're the shrinks here. You need to talk to us."

She pauses.

"Maybe you'll see one next week, but nothing's certain."

They can drop dead, I won't talk to them. I'll wait for the shrink.

Fortunately, the kids on my floor are nice. Most of them don't have eating disorders. They've made suicide attempts or have other personal difficulties. Some have scars on their arms. One of them, who has a long braid running down her back, scratches her skin until it bleeds. I'd never seen anything like it.

Little Ronan, who is 7, has recurring fits of anger. I've rarely seen him go through one of these phases. He's always sweet and gentle. His eyes are blue and wide open.

When his behavior changes, the nurses grab him by the arms and take him to a room called the "expression room", where there's a punching bag.—where there's a punching bag suspended by a chain and children's writing on the walls. I can hear him screaming and crying in the distance, and I feel very sorry for him.

I'm also very fond of Aline, a 15-year-old girl who has the peculiarity of fainting at any moment. Sitting or standing. She's very caring, and I think of her as a big sister, confiding in her at difficult times.

Finally, there's Léana, a young girl with bulimia. She's slim, but more shapely than Hélie and me. She has a special, bewitching voice. Her eyes terrify me. I don't understand her lack of control over food. *How is it possible to swallow such quantities of food and then be vomited on without being sure you've got it all out of your body? It's dirty and frightening.* Unlike me and Hélie, Léana is allowed to do cooking workshops. When she bakes cookies, a sweet fragrance wafts through the floor.

With the hospitalized children, we sometimes gather in a circle near the bay window of the communal living area.

"I think they should let us out once in a while. I feel even sadder than before I came back here," says Ronan.

"I agree with you, they should give us a taste for life, rather than damaging us even more."

I'm looking forward to my parents' first visit. Prostrate in front of my bedroom window. The minutes are long, my gaze fixed on the road around the corner from the parking lot. I dream of seeing my parents' car there. I imagine it very loudly in my thoughts.

When I finally see them arrive, I jump for joy and wave to them from behind my bedroom window. After a while, their eyes catch the window. They smile at me and, after 5 minutes, reach the floor.

"Your parents are here, Oihana, you can join them. You can go downstairs to the parking lot. An hour, no more."

I jump into their arms and descend the steps in the joy of being back outside—the air, the sun, and the sounds of the city.

We sit down by the front steps. I begin to tell my parents about the pain of my daily life in this new hospital. The unkindness of the nurses, the confinement in the rooms, the overloaded plates, the constant heaviness of life shared with very damaged people.

I also explain that I was being watched by a nurse during the call we'd had two days earlier. I wasn't free to tell them how I really felt, because my words are reported to the doctors.

I begged my parents to take me home with them.

"I'll make an effort, I promise."

My parents understand my suffering, and hug me. It feels good, less alone.

"We'll try to talk to them when we get back up."

Mrs. Brisset is the doctor in charge of the unit.

My father looks gently in my direction, then turns to the medical team.

"How can we explain to her that it's for her own good that she has to stay here?"

Mrs. Brisset glances dismissively at her charts, then replies, completely missing the point:

"It wasn't with us that she fell ill... But with you."

A silence settled over the small consulting room. My father, usually a strong-tempered man, was speechless, taken aback.

To lighten the mood, my mother continues:

"Can she at least go outside for a few minutes a day, accompanied by a carer?"

"No, the rules are the same for all our patients. Outings are granted at certain stages of care only."

My mother then negotiated for me to keep a small plant in my room, which would give a little life to the space in which I was confined. At first, the doctors refused.

"Decorative objects are forbidden, as they can hide medicines, sharp objects or food."

After a few minutes of discussion, they finally relented. I get the right to have a plant in my room, thanks to my mother. The planter is magnificent. It's pink and silver, adorned with tiny blue diamonds. My little brother and my mother decorated it.

I say goodbye to my parents from my bedroom window.

My father has come up with a trick to make me feel less lonely. We set our watches together, down to the second. And every evening, at 8.50 p.m., we make a date to meet.

It's the only time of day when I smile.

*

The days go by. Hélie makes progress on the piece she practices tirelessly on the piano, *Comptine d'un autre été*, by Yann Tiersen. She can now play the fast passage, with its magnificent melody. Her haunting repetitions mark every day of my hospitalization.

I promise myself to watch the film from which the song is taken as soon as I leave hospital: *Amélie Poulain*.

A nurse takes me to a small room where she weighs me: 41.5 kg.

My efforts are paying off, but the rising numbers scare the hell out of me. It's never going to stop.

"The probe will be removed tomorrow. You'll join the communal meals."

I'm delighted, because this step towards food autonomy seemed out of reach. It's another step towards leaving the hospital. However, I feel that my progress is only on the surface. It's an illusion, a perfectly staged staging, to convince the carers to let me go home—while protecting *The Voice.*

Every day, *She* holds me in a constant, oppressive embrace. Every moment, *She* reminds me that eating is synonymous with weight gain, fatigue and lack of willpower.

After three months of nasogastric tube feeding, I can finally breathe through both nostrils. I can move freely in bed at night, without fear of tearing out the connecting cable.

Group meals are a living hell. I'm under constant surveillance. My every move is analyzed.

When I go to the dining room, I pass Hélie's door, who is eating alone, facing the wall of her room. I feel sad to see her helpless in front of her meal tray, her back slightly bent.

There are eight of us seated around a large rectangular table—seven patients and one care assistant. Two dishes overflowing with dubious preparations sit in the middle of the table. *Those damn cauliflowers full of fat again! They really only have one recipe here.*

"You must help yourself, Oihana."

I help myself to a ladleful of each dish. The orderly bores her eyes into mine.

"It's not enough."

It's not fair. The children opposite me have less on their plates. The nurse's aide stands up and makes way for a man in his twenties, with light, straight hair, who enters the room with a tray of slices of white ham in his hands.

"Mathias will take care of eating with you today."

The orderly turns to me.

"Oihana, you must take two slices."

I can't stand their two slices! *Nobody eats two slices of ham in one meal.* The nurse leaves the room. My neck bends, my gaze falls on my plate. I feel sad and upset. My fingers struggle to grasp the cutlery.

Suddenly, a foreign hand grabs one of the two slices of ham on my plate. I look up, Mathias winks at me as he swallows my slice of ham. He then brings his index finger up to his mouth with a smile, signalling me to keep this secret to myself.

This gesture might seem unprofessional to some, but for me it was a tender interlude in a day-to-day life where I felt alone and misunderstood. A slice of ham more or less wouldn't have had much impact on my weight gain, but this moment of complicity gave me strength for the days ahead.

*

The monotonous weeks are interspersed with a few group activities, written on a board near the common room: ping-pong tournament in the hospital basement, visit to the Bordeaux botanical gardens.

In the middle of each outing, we are obliged to have a snack, around 4 p.m. I choose a briquette of strawberry-flavored milk and savor it slowly. Each new flavor provokes an ecstasy in my mouth. I close my eyes and rediscover one of the sweet flavors that lulled my childhood. Unfortunately, fear and guilt soon overtake me. *A snack? What's next? You already eat enough at mealtimes.*

*

Today, we're taking part in an art workshop in a small room off the unit's common room. The facilitator asks us to illustrate a dream.

An idea comes to me very quickly. I start drawing the ocean on a large sheet of paper, a powerful, magnificent blue. Above the horizon, an elongated island, slightly bulging on the right side: Izaro. This island faces Bermeo—the town in the Spanish Basque country from which my maternal grandmother came, and where I spent a large part of my childhood.

I stand up and take two steps back to check that the composition of my drawing is correct. Fred, the nurse who had refused to let me call my parents on the first evening, gives me a murderous look.

"Sit down."

He's awful, useless, depressive. He should be institutionalized, not us.

*

Every morning after breakfast, it's the medicine round, and a few times a week, the doctors' round. We have to sit in our beds, waiting for the medical team to enter our rooms.

Suddenly, I find myself surrounded by two nurses, a male nurse, three young interns and Mrs. Brisset. I feel judged, analyzed, like a captive animal. The attraction of a human zoo. The laboratory rat.

Mrs. Brisset comments aloud, as if I weren't there. The interns take notes while Fred, the nurse I detest, leans against the medicine cabinet and passively observes the wall behind me. As useless as ever.

Mrs. Brisset takes two steps in my direction, then points to my feet:

"You see? She has no socks. The perfect example of an anorexic looking to burn calories by any means necessary!"

I'm stunned by what Mrs. Brisset has just said. I've loved going barefoot at home ever since I was little, because socks give me a feeling of compression. But not because I'm looking to cool my body down for may grir. I hate the cold. It's the middle of May, and I'm allowed to go barefoot in bed! I keep this thought to myself, and remain immersed in silence. I know I won't be heard, no matter what.

Following this medical interview, a nurse comes into my room to massage the bedsores on my lower back, caused by bed rest.

This afternoon, I see my parents again. I've been granted permission to go into town. We're off to the miroir d'eau, an iconic Bordeaux landmark that I loved discovering on a school trip last year.

I can't wait to show it off to my parents. Unfortunately, when we get there, there's no water—the ground is perfectly dry. So we sit down for a moment, facing the Garonne, and talk.

The distance from my family and the feeling of imprisonment are becoming unbearable. I'm fed up with not being able to move around wherever I want. I'm tired of being spied on all the time, in my most intimate moments. Not being allowed to sit down or stand up without a caregiver's permission. To live in constant fear of "doing the wrong thing", and having my hospitalization extended for bad behavior. Not to enjoy the simple pleasure of opening my windows to breathe the fresh morning air.

We then head for a bar where I'm obliged to have a snack—a clementine and a yoghurt—as it's 4 p.m., and the nurses have given my parents this instruction.

We sit down around a table and continue chatting. Suddenly, I break down. Tears spill down my cheeks. A feeling of helplessness and anger grows in my chest. I stand up, annoyed by the situation, annoyed by the furloughs, annoyed by the solitude I'll find again tonight. With quick steps, I head for the bathroom and lock myself in. Then I shout:

"I can't take this anymore! I'm never going back to that prison! I'm staying right here. Leave me alone... I'd rather die here."

I fall to the floor and sit up, my arms wrapped around my legs, the side of my head pressed against my knees. I cry continuously. Then I close my eyes. My anger subsides, I say no more.

On the other side of the door, my mother tries to reassure me. When I don't answer, she gets worried and says, in a trembling voice:

"Please, Oihana..."

The pain in her voice makes me react. I don't have to put them through this, on top of everything they're already going through. I open the door.

Then we go back to the hospital.

At night, as I lie in bed, I think back to my early childhood. How could I have fallen so far, when everything was so wonderful?

*

This lunchtime, Hélie joins the communal meals. It's the first time I've sat down with a person suffering from anorexia.

She's seated opposite me, next to Aline—the young girl who regularly collapses. A nurse places veal cutlets and a tray of fried potatoes in the middle of the table. I watch Hélie out of the corner of my eye, trying to catch his reactions. Her eyes are weary and evasive, plunged into her still-empty plate. I hope she's all right.

Fortunately, children who don't have eating disorders have light-hearted discussions that lighten the mood.

Aline is laughing with Ronan, when suddenly her eyes roll back. She falls from her chair and faints, the cutlery in her hand ricocheting off the floor. Fortunately, the nurses react quickly. Aline is usually so smiley, it's hard to see her in this state.

After this disconcerting scene, we continue our therapeutic meal. I argue with *The Voice* as I chew my veal escalope. It's to get us out of here, I promise.

The hard part done, we move on to dessert. A yoghurt—*high in sugar and fat*—is served. Hélie grabs her dessert with her slender fingertips. She then dips the back of her teaspoon into the surface of her yoghurt and consumes it, gently lapping it up in a gripping slowness.

I feel as if a mirror is being held up to me. Hélie's gestures echo my own, as if borrowed from me. This reflection destabilizes me.

After dinner, I drag myself to my room and sit in bed, my back to the wall, my legs bent. A child from the unit cries out in the distance—I don't recognize his voice.

I feel nothing. Neither sadness nor anger. Just a feeling of intense emptiness.

I open a letter written by Laura, my friend from college. Here's an excerpt:

> *In my diary, I have marked every day since you left with a red line. From the evening of February 19 until today. We all think of you at school. People often ask us, "Have you heard from Oihana?" To which I reply that you have gone to Bordeaux. I send you big kisses full of energy. I adore you.* Laura

Return

June 2013, 13 years

A week ago, the medical team at the psychiatric hospital announced my discharge date: June 7, 2013. At this meeting, Mrs. Brisset was unexpressive and distant, punctuating only certain exchanges with detached comments:

"Anyway, she's not making any progress."

The days leading up to this announcement had been very difficult. Every morning, I woke up with fear in my stomach, dazzled by the cold neon light in my bedroom. The bouts of tears and anger intensified day after day, each passing minute more painful than the last. Repeatedly telling my parents that staying here would destroy me further, they finally gave in and applied for an early discharge—against medical advice. I sensed that this was a very difficult decision for them to make. So I did my best to reassure them about what would happen next, but the fear that I would relapse once I was discharged hung over us like a silent threat.

One hundred and five days have passed since my admission to pediatrics, thirty-two of which were spent in psychiatry. I don't realize that I'm about to regain my freedom. The very idea of being able to walk wherever I want, at any time of day, seems unreal to me. I can't wait to return to the colorful flowers of my childhood garden, the birdsong and the tinkling of my village bell.

I smile at the thought as I stand in front of the bay window of the communal living area. My luggage is ready, grouped together at the foot of my armchair. Aline, Hélie and Ronan sit beside me, silently sharing in my happiness. I can see in their eyes an urgent desire to escape, in their turn, from this sad pavilion where time seems to have stood still.

"That's it, it's your turn today. You're in luck... Take advantage of us outside, we'll miss you."

The idea of leaving them locked within these walls squeezes my heart. I feel like I'm abandoning them, and dread not hearing from them again.

I watch the road leading to the hospital parking lot for a long time, my eyes catching every movement on the street. I dream of seeing my parents' truck appear, its faded red body a perfect contrast to the gray of the facades. Half an hour has already passed since the announced time of arrival . My smile is gradually fading. What if they'd forgotten me? What if the release date had been postponed without my knowledge? I won't last another day here.

Fortunately, almost an hour later, the truck of my childhood appears at the bend in the road. As I catch sight of it, the smell of linoleum and wet sand that characterizes it comes to me as if by magic. I imagine the sound of the music that used to set the rhythm of our vacations. A wave of happiness washes over me as I catch a glimpse of my brothers' silhouettes, hidden by the reflection of the windows.

The truck stops, the doors open. My parents get out and wave, smiling. As they join me on the landing, the loneliness that had been gnawing at me for weeks leaves me. I feel instantly relieved. They help me cross the corridor for the last time, carrying my suitcases. I'm happy to be surrounded by my loved ones again.

As we approach the hospital exit, we see Mrs. Brisset. She shakes my father's hand and says: "You'll see, you'll be back."

*

The first few days out of hospital were frightening. I no longer have any reference points in my childhood home. The fear of losing control and being institutionalized again hangs over me without ceasing. To reassure my parents that they were right to discharge me from hospital, I try to keep up with the pace of family life. I sit with them, in silence, even if meals are difficult. I try to keep up with the TV shows we used to watch together, but my mind wanders. I can't concentrate on anything but the food.

Sometimes I go for walks with my parents, but physical activity has been exhausting me since I got out of hospital. I think back to the childhood pleasures of walks in the forest, conquering wild blackberries, eyes raised to the treetops. But now, the warmth of the sun and the song of the birds only awaken in me a deep melancholy.

This weariness extends to my social interactions, with every conversation requiring an immense effort. I feel completely disconnected from reality. Communication with my brothers—who are now both teenagers—has become almost impossible. Their interests no longer match mine, and I can no longer open up to them. Nothing makes me laugh any more, and words and topics of conversation are hard to come by. My body struggles to keep up with the family spirit.

The changes in my relationship with my loved ones affect me enormously. I'm no longer the sister or daughter they once knew. I'm afraid I've broken something between us for good.

Despite this inner suffering, I'm trying to make progress and resist *The Voice,* which is as present as ever. My parents make sure that I don't repeat the OCD that haunted me before my hospitalization. They accompany me to the most striking places in the house—such as the staircase, where I used to go up and down three out of twenty-one steps, before tumbling down the whole thing. For the first time in nine months, I go down the stairs normally, one step at a time, all the way to the end, accompanied by my father. It's working, I'm managing to detach myself from certain rituals, even if *She* tugs at my heartstrings with each confrontation.

We also take down all the sports and fashion posters that used to hang on my bedroom wall. When I detach the one of the woman I used to compare myself with before being hospitalized, I'm torn between a sense of pride and the fear of disappointing *The Voice. She* freezes every limb of my body and echoes in my head. *This woman was your example, what will become of you if you no longer resemble her?* Fortunately, for once, I manage to focus on my parents' smile. I fold the poster into quarters and insert it into a binder, which I place on the highest shelf of my bedroom cupboard, among other anorexia-related objects and books I've also put away—like diet manuals, drawings I've made during hospitalizations and calorie-tracking notebooks.

The Voice manages to turn the situation to her advantage. *You don't need all those tools now, it's all in your head.*

*

As they had promised, my parents gave me a wonderful present when I left hospital: a little dog that we adopted from the SPA in Mont-de-Marsan on June 21. She's only a few months old, black, very small and slender. We named her Alaia—which means "joyful" in Basque. I love her dearly and hope, deep down, that she will give me the strength and desire to heal.

One day on vacation, while I was walking her by a lake, Alaia pulled on the leash and knocked me over, dragging me a few meters along the ground, under the astonished gazes of all the people enjoying the beach. Alaia is small and light, but she has much more strength than I do.

My brothers and I laughed a lot about this scene. These moments of rediscovered complicity soothe me a little.

Unfortunately, even Alaia's presence isn't enough to calm my torments. Today, as thoughts of food gnawed at me, I plunged my head into Alaia's packet of kibbles and sniffed it thoroughly, entranced by that very special smell.

A shiver of shame ran through my body as I returned to my room. "*You're just an animal,*" *The Voice* keeps telling me.

*

A few weeks after leaving the hospital, I learn that the principal of my middle school has agreed to let me move up to the next level, despite my absence last term.

To make up for the three months I'd missed, I sat down every day at the end of my family's dining room table and toiled for hours on end. The photocopies of lessons all look the same to me. Words get jumbled. Mathematical rules are incomprehensible. *The Voice* grows impatient in my head. *You see, you're no longer capable of anything.*

My math teacher, Monsieur Créteau, very kindly offers to give me remedial lessons at home. He's patient and pedagogical, which allows me to catch up without losing heart. I really appreciate the time he gives me.

Since I've been home from hospital, I feel surrounded and supported. The mother of one of my childhood friends, Michelle, sometimes comes to the house to give me a massage. She treats my body with gentleness and respect, despite my thinness. While she massages me, we talk at length, on a variety of subjects. These intimate, enriching exchanges make me feel like a person in my own right, not reduced to anorexia.

*

July 26, 2013. My feet land one after the other on the cold surface of the scale. 41.6 kg, almost 2 kg lighter since my release from the psychiatric hospital. *The Voice* is reassured, but doesn't react any further. *She* abandons me when the anxiety of being hospitalized overwhelms me, or when I'm afraid of losing weight endlessly, until my body gives out.

Since I've been discharged from hospital, Mrs. Roger and Mrs. Leclerc have been keeping a very close eye on me. Every appointment at the Maison des Adolescents is an oppressive ordeal. Will my weight match the scale this morning? What will Mrs. Roger think of my weight loss? At every appointment, every gram, every word, every gesture is evaluated. I'm exhausted by this constant monitoring.

"You need to stabilize," Mrs. Roger keeps telling me. *The Voice* doesn't balk when *She* hears these words. The term "stabilize" is less frightening than "get fat", "gain weight", "shape weight", "healthy weight".

Fortunately, when I cross the threshold of the Maison des Adolescents, the secretary always gives me a warm welcome. Her sincere smile and cheerful voice soothe me as soon as I enter the room. My parents also do their utmost to support me during these difficult appointments, waiting in the waiting room during each consultation, and taking the time to chat with me on the way home. I don't want to disappoint them. My biggest fear is that Mrs. Roger will scare them away from me.

So, on the days when I dread losing weight, I use a trick my family doctor inadvertently informed me about:

"I had an anorexic patient a few years ago... On weigh-in days, she would drink up to two liters of water before consultations so that it would show on the scale. What a technique! Can you believe it?"

The Voice was quick to take note. But, unfortunately, Mrs. Roger knows every conceivable ploy used by anorexics. The water technique works once or twice, but no more. Mrs. Roger soon caught on. One day, she confided in me, almost as a warning:

"Did you go to the bathroom before the weigh-in? I'm used to it, you know... I even have anorexic patients who load their pockets with heavy objects..."

Mrs. Roger wants me to be honest with her, above all. But I can't do it completely. I want her to be proud of me too. In her absence, during my stay in a psychiatric hospital, I realized how much she meant to me.

One day, when I got up, I felt the need to give shape to everything that was going through me. So I began work on a little illustrated book about anorexia: *Je voulais juste voler (I just wanted to fly). The Voice* accompanies me in the creation of each page. Every sentence has to be clean and punchy. Every drawing must be precise and flawless. As the project nears completion, I rush through it, eager to see how it looks in print. *The last two pages don't look right. You really don't know how to draw clouds. The Voice* makes me pronounce my book's defects orally:

"The positions of the flying character are all wrong. And it's a bit silly too..."

Fortunately, my mother, who helps and supports me in my artistic projects, reassures me and silences *The Voice*. She holds out the book at the end of her arms, and says with a smile:

"I don't agree. It's a beautiful book!"

She's the one who took the time to print and bind it. I often blame myself, because I'm hard on my mother when I'm afraid she'll crumple one of my drawings when she grabs it, or when one of my projects doesn't turn out as I'd imagined. She's never at fault, quite the contrary. She's always patient, a good listener, takes the time to think of ideas to help me, and gives up her time to teach me new techniques. I, on the other hand, am incapable of dealing with my own frustrations, cowardly blaming those I love the most.

Despite the few flaws in my little book, I decide to present it to Mrs. Roger at a follow-up appointment. My heart races as I hand it to her. Fortunately, it soon becomes clear that she's interested in the project, from the expression that gradually appears on her face. Her eyes light up as she turns the pages. Certain sentences seem to capture her attention. At the end of the reading, Mrs. Roger asks me if she can present my booklet at a meeting on eating disorders. I'm delighted at the idea. So I bring her other drawings, made before and during the hospitalization. She takes the time to observe each one with great care.

The attention she pays to my creations touches me deeply and gives meaning to what I'm going through.

Despite these isolated moments of joy, the summer passed slowly, without much sparkle. Every day is an ordeal, marked by weariness and exhaustion. Setting up creative projects takes a lot of energy. I rarely read, write or draw. When I express my sadness, my mother asks me:

"Is there anything you used to enjoy? Could we go for a walk, or to the movies?"

I'm very surprised not to find an answer to this question. I don't feel like doing anything anymore. What's become of me?

The sun is burning outside, yet the cold continues to gnaw at my bones.

*

Back to school in 4th.

I rediscover the place where I collapsed six months earlier. Every nook and cranny reminds me of the OCD, the cold and the tears.

In the rows, middle-schoolers holler and hustle. *The chicken coop.* I nearly fall over at every touch. One of the students grabs my hat and throws it across the yard, giggling. I watch the scene from outside, not having the strength to retrieve it. The piercing sound of ringing pierces my chest and clouds my thoughts.

Fortunately, Laura, the friend who supported me last year, is in my class. Her presence is an anchor. Her words help me to connect with the present moment, as my thoughts are constantly wandering. I'm constantly thinking about the children who were in the psychiatric hospital with me. How are they? Their screams and cries still echo in my head. Their bruised eyes and injured forearms appear to me as soon as I close my eyes.

I'm struggling to find any interest in the fact that Jessica stole Theo, Lucie's lover. I'm exasperated by the discussion topics of the people in my class.

Fortunately, Laura is very intelligent and gentle. She treats me the same way she did before my illness. She teases me and protects me. I always stay by her side.

*

My parents think it's important for me to stay active. So I take up basketball again.

After a nine-month break, I return to the gym and the team I left so abruptly, with the sensation of arriving in unfamiliar territory. The smell of the gym, the crunch of shoes and the constant pounding of the balls seem foreign to me, as if they belong to another life. I no longer have any reflexes, the ball constantly slipping out of my hands. My shots no longer reach the hoop. My dribbling is no longer coordinated. During every one-on-one exercise, I lose my balance. My opponents easily snatch the ball out of my hands. The slightest physical contact sends me crashing to the ground. Nothing feels natural anymore. The girls in my team react dynamically to every action, while my eyes remain fixed in the void.

I've lost my complicity with some of my teammates and a few of the adults in the club. Sometimes, during training sessions or team outings, former girlfriends form groups just a few metres away from me, laughing loudly and excluding me from discussions when I try to join in. Fortunately, the players' parents and some of the girls, such as Laeticia, Morgane and Bénédicte, treat me with tenderness and respect, as if nothing had changed between us.

From the very first basketball game, I lose my role as point guard and the number on my jersey: 9. I spend most of my time on the bench. I feel ashamed when my parents come to see me when I'm so little on the court, or worse, when I miss simple actions. *You've really gone to shit," The Voice* keeps telling me.

I think back to when I was hard on the girls on my team. I blame myself.

The years of anorexia have taught me humility and empathy.

*

My parents gave me a cell phone so I can contact them when I'm feeling down at school. I spend a lot of recess locked in the toilets, exchanging text messages with my father.

"What's your resume like?"

"Hard, very cold. Tough math test this morning. I want to go home..."

“Come on, only a few more hours to go and we’re together. We’ll be fine! Jtm”

Some evenings, I text Laura or Louis—a nice, funny boy in my class.

We talk at length, he tries to understand me and sometimes manages to put a smile on my face.

One day, Louis confided his feelings to me. I wasn’t ready to receive such information and didn’t know how to react. How can you get attached to someone who’s skinny, sad and out of touch with the real world?

All the same, the news did cheer me up at a very special time in my life. I’ll never forget it.

*

After several months of college struggling to keep up, I cracked again. From the moment I open my eyes in the morning, I’m petrified of facing a new day, boarding school transport where everyone is bustling, enduring endless hours of lessons, long recesses in the cold, noisy meals in the canteen.

The most difficult days are those when I have basketball practice in the evening. I spend the day dreading the physical exercises that await me in the multi-purpose room—whose broken windows let in cold draughts. Will I be able to cope with the social interaction and the demands of tonight’s workout? How many layers of clothing should I wear to protect myself from the intense cold? Will I be able to do my homework properly when I get home? I don’t know how I’m going to manage.

My academic perfectionism isn't compatible with leisure activities and the development of social relationships. I'm completely lost.

After much thought and discussion with my parents, the idea of distance education came to me. Our family doctor accepted this choice without passing judgment. Accompanied by my parents, I went through the registration process. With each form I filled in, I got closer to a more serene everyday life.

A few weeks later, I discover a delivery notice in my family's mailbox. My heart races. It could be the CNED (Centre national d'enseignement à distance) parcel waiting for me at my village post office! I quickly get ready, put on a suitable outfit and rush out the door. When I arrive at the counter, the postmistress points to a huge cardboard box on the counter. The parcel is heavy and hard to carry, yet I feel light, almost euphoric. Relieved at the idea of finally leaving the painful daily grind of school.

As soon as I get home, I hurriedly pounce on the parcel and discover, inside, a number of thick exercise books, sorted by color and subject. I'm impressed by the sheer volume of these books. "*We're going to make it,*" *The Voice* whispers to me. *You don't need anyone to finish your year.*

The CNED

March 2014, age 13

Since I've been home-schooled, I've lived in close cohabitation with *The Voice*. Once again, *she*'s my only interlocutor. Every gesture, every action in my daily life is dictated by its orders.

My weight stagnates at 44 kg. I still haven't got my period back. When *she* speaks to me more frequently, large quantities of hair fall from my head. This external symptom allows me to detect relapses and take action before the situation worsens.

Paradoxically, I feel calmer now that I'm out of school. My social interactions are limited to my family, when they come home from work in the evening, and some of the girls in my basketball club.

Fortunately, for some time now, I've been maintaining a letter-writing relationship with my college friend Laura.

Here are a few extracts from letters she's sent me:

"I so wish you could have been with us at the end of the year. We're becoming good friends with the boys, and we laugh a lot. [...]

As the art teacher said to me: now, Laura, you're an orphan. You no longer have Oihana."

"Why did I choose this card? Well, I think this snowman looks strangely like you, with his hat, his big scarf, his sweater and his gloves! But above all, you have the same nose, which reddens when it's cold! Isn't he a handsome little snowman?"

"The leafless tree on this card shows that winter is devastating everything. But the rosy blue sky means that spring is just around the corner..."

"Persisting in writing to each other and using this outdated mode of communication for some, reminds me of that time when we were out of step with others."

"I'm reading a philosophical book, a bit heady, but full of wisdom and reason: Sophie's World. *I enclose this quote:*

'What is the most important thing in life? All men need food, of course. And also love and tenderness. But there's something else we all need: to know who we are and why we live.'"

*

Alongside the hours of relentless schoolwork, I take refuge in a creative world that occupies all my mind. I pencil, paint, cut, sculpt, glue and write whenever I have a moment. I spend hours researching new creative tutorials, exploring new techniques, preparing productions for drawing, comic strip and writing competitions. Every victory, no matter how small, gives me a boost of pride, while every defeat feeds criticism from *The Voice. You didn't apply yourself hard enough. It shows in this part of the drawing.*

I'm sinking into an obsessive, marginal daily routine. Every day is exactly the same, from the moment I get up to the moment I go to bed. Every calorie is counted. Every food is weighed. Every nook and cranny of my body is carefully monitored. Nothing must stick out. The touch of my bones always reassures *The Voice.*

At least you're capable of that.

*

In May 2014, our family and I are invited to the 45th birthday party of Hervé, a long-time friend of my parents. I consider Hervé and his wife Caroline members of my family. They've watched me grow up since I was 2 years old. Their daughter, Chloé, is a year older than me. I think of her as my sister.

Her family moved to the city two years ago. Since then, it's become difficult to see each other. I haven't seen Chloé or her family since I fell into anorexia. I dread their reactions to the changes in my body and personality.

When we arrive at their new apartment, I'm overwhelmed by a feeling of happiness. Hervé and Caroline welcome me with tenderness, kindness and cheerfulness. Nothing has changed.

Chloé smiles at me and takes me up to her room, where we chat for hours and laugh, just like when we were little.

She makes no remarks about my looks, and understands everything I say. We talk about the two years we've spent apart. I've missed her terribly.

The Voice makes me suffer so much that my nostalgia for my childhood is multiplied tenfold. But Chloé reassures me and keeps me connected to the present, as well as to the lightness of adolescence. In the months and years to come, she's the only person outside my family with whom I've shared evenings, vacations and moments of complicity.

Her door remained wide open, despite the sadness and emptiness I felt. I can't thank her enough for that.

*

September 2014, I've completed my 4th year at the CNED and am about to start 3rd grade. As agreed with my parents, I'm changing schools. I'm thrilled at the idea of this new beginning. On the eve of the start of the new school year, I carefully prepare an outfit that I feel comfortable in.

Unfortunately, my hopes were dashed within the first few hours I spent here. I soon missed the safe, creative space I'd built for myself at the CNED. I couldn't fit in with the other students, who had certainly been together for several years.

I spend several breaks alone in the playground, with the feeling that certain people are staring at me.

Lunch in the cafeteria is very difficult. I sit with two girls from my class whom I hardly know. They're nice, but every smile seems like an ordeal. We chat about shallow subjects:

"Have you seen Enzo in 3rd B?"

"The one who hangs out with the popular kids?"

"Yes, I have! Don't you think he looks better than he did before the summer?"

The Voice is totally uninterested in this conversation, raising her voice so loudly in my head that I can't follow what's being said. *What a waste of time... You'd be better off devoting yourself to work and creation.* I sink into my thoughts. I miss Laura. She made me feel good.

Throughout the meal, I do my best not to let my eating problems show. I force myself not to cut my portion of fish into too small pieces, so as to appear normal. Chewing each mouthful is an effort. I swallow the fish piece by piece, with difficulty, with the sensation of swallowing pebbles.

After a week, I begged my parents to let me continue this year at the CNED. Faced with so much suffering, they agreed, albeit with major reservations about prolonged isolation and the role the disease could play if I were left alone with it for too long.

When I received the package from the CNED, I couldn't be completely happy. Despite my new-found serenity, I see this situation as a failure, a step backwards. Laura writes to me:

You know, I understand that your start at the CNED was "complicated", to use your words, but I sincerely think it's better for you, in hindsight. It's not that you're not "academic", on the contrary, I think you're a true artist who has to let herself be guided by her flow of inspiration. To have to bend to a timetable, like in high school, instead of organizing yourself according to your artistic impulses, would be to spoil your immense talent and prevent it from developing.

New fears arise in me about the brevet des collèges. I do some research on the Internet and discover a study that confirms my worries:

"The percentage of pupils taking the brevet des collèges who are free candidates is 59.1%, compared with 86.8% for traditional schoolchildren. For the bac général, 49.6% for cnédiens versus 92.7% for lycéens."

Despite the fear, I promise myself I'll succeed. I'll do everything I can to pass the brevet des collèges on my own. *And with honors,"* adds *The Voice.*

It's the start of a year of transition, marked by a return to solitude and the firmness of my new organization. My rhythm of life shifted considerably. I work every day from noon to midnight, to be precise. Twelve hours in front of my classes, with no respite. *The Voice* doesn't allow me to take vacations or weekends. I work non-stop, seven days a week. *You have to make the most of every moment to progress and get the "Très bien" grade.* Fortunately, I enjoy immersing myself in the learning of every notion on the syllabus. I explore my CNED courses, read articles on the Internet and watch documentaries. I focus on each subject over several days, to have time to understand everything. Four days of history. Two days of mathematics. Three days of life and earth sciences. I peel back certain subjects for hours, looking for the smallest detail that escapes me. *The Voice* is delighted by this intellectual emulation. *She* is particularly interested in certain subjects—such as French, history and art, which *she* considers noble and poetic. Work monopolizes my mind. Day and night, I'm visited by the characters I discover as I read.

The CNED operates an exchange platform between teachers and students. I have to send in assignments by certain dates. Even though I don't know my teachers in real life, I can imagine their personalities through the comments they give me in writing.

From midnight to 5 a.m., *The Voice* allows me to rest. I take advantage of this time to watch animated films, and perfect my culture in this field. Every night, I immerse myself in the remarkable worlds of my favorite directors—Hayao Miyazaki, Tomm Moore and Michel Ocelot—and scour the Internet for documentaries on their life stories. By registering on the "SensCritique" site, I discover the variety of animation styles and studios, through lists of recommendations devised by Internet users. Each film I discover transports me into a dream. I imagine myself crossing the green fields of the Japanese countryside, accompanied by Satsuki from *My Neighbor Totoro*. My journey continues through the majestic landscapes of *Kirikou* and *Azur et Asmar,* where every detail is tinged with flamboyant colors. At the end of this journey, I settle into the *Tales of the Night* theater, where I enjoy the poetry of stories from different cultures.

But animation isn't just a way of escaping, it's also an extraordinary means of conveying lessons and emotions to people of all ages. For these reasons, *The Voice* is particularly fond of this field.

Luckily, my mother accompanies me in this passion. We both go to the cinema to discover the latest animated film releases. During screenings, the noise of people eating popcorn disgusts me and detracts from the magic of the experience. *They're awful and eat like pigs.* Fortunately, the best cinemas, which mainly show independent studio films, don't offer popcorn at the door.

On the way back, we spend long minutes debriefing the films we've just discovered. I love these moments of sharing with my mother, away from my day-to-day work. I feel less alone and understood.

*

Every morning at the CNED starts the same way. I walk down the steps to the dining room, in a silent, mechanical habit, and greet our little dog Alaia, who watches me intently from her basket. The perceptible sound of the clock indicates that the house is empty—stripped of the music and children's laughter that once inhabited it.

Every day of the week, without exception, I place the laptop I'm working with on the kitchen bar. This allows me to stand while keeping the screen at eye level. *The Voice* forbids me to sit down during my working day. *It's bad enough you live a sedentary life, but you're not going to slouch in a chair all day either.* Twelve hours on my feet. I'm not allowed to relax, either physically or mentally.

When I travel alone to the Spanish Basque Country to work at my grandmother's house, I put my CNED textbook or a novel on the syllabus on a shelf at eye level, so that I can leaf through the book while ingesting the nourishment *The Voice* grants me.

After months of standing, the blood no longer flows properly through my legs. At the end of the day, a pain pulses through my shins and calves. So I walk around the family dining table, notebook in hand, to get the blood flowing. In the evening, I raise the bottom of my bed to make my legs hurt less.

When I color my drawings on the family computer, which sits on a low desk, it's hard to see the whole screen. So I push aside the chair—forbidden by *The Voice*—and kneel on the floor, maintaining this position for hours: my back straight and my gaze fixed on my drawing, which is slowly coming into focus. By dint of holding myself like this every day, my knees become covered in red patches, injured by the wear and tear of the floor. My close friends and my maternal and paternal family witness these scenes, powerless in the face of such self-destruction. If a single person has the misfortune to come to my aid in this situation, *The Voice* becomes exasperated:

“Leave me alone. I know very well what I’m doing.”

The chair is forbidden. The Voice inflicted this rule on me for several years.

*

My diet has become tighter since I started distance learning. My new organization has become so extensive that I no longer share my meals with my nearest and dearest. A slight feeling of sadness sometimes comes over me when I hear or see my family gathered around the daily dinner—where tongues are loosened and bonds forged. Part of me would like to join them, to join in their discussions and laugh in their company, but the other part prefers calm, solitude, control and the cult of work. *You have so much to do... The Voice* reminds me.

My daily diet follows an increasingly strict and singular logic. When I wake up, all I eat is 0% raspberry yoghurt—this flavor and no other, since it’s my favorite and guarantees a moment of pleasure during the shortest meal of the day.

At 2.17 p.m., I enjoy three 0% fruit yogurts in the following order: apricot, blackberry, raspberry. Fifteen minutes per yoghurt minimum. Lunch has to be over by 3 p.m. at the earliest—the intervals without food have to be as short as possible so that my body and mind don’t feel the withdrawal. I use exactly the same model of teaspoon to eat yoghurt, as its lightness and shape are perfectly suited to my way of consuming it.

My dinner starts at 7.17 p.m. and lasts for several hours. This meal accounts for the remainder of the 1,500 kcal I consume daily. I deliberately condense most of my intake in the evening so that I feel full at least once a day, and don't go to bed hungry. During these dinner hours, I stand in front of my class. My eyes are fixed on my computer screen, where a multitude of texts scroll by. My fingers articulate nervously on the keyboard keys, then settle around the various foods I'm eating: steamed eggplants and broccoli, sliced chicken ham, cherry tomatoes, 0% yoghurts, wholemeal bread, flavored milks (which I froth so that the air fills me up even more and the tasting lasts longer). Some solid foods are cut into small pieces and eaten with Asian chopsticks—which allow me to eat precisely and slow down the eating process.

The Voice controls everything I eat. Food is meticulously weighed on a kitchen scale. Every calorie is recorded in a scientific calculator—which has the advantage of a built-in history. No more need for my calorie book. Dietary programs may vary throughout the year, but the basis remains the same.

I also drink large quantities of sugar-free soft drinks, to compensate for the lack of food during the day. These beverages cause considerable sensitivity in my teeth and stomach.

*

My little dog, Alaia, accompanies me in this solitary daily routine. She keeps an eye on me all day long, perks up her ears at the slightest noise that disturbs the silence of the house, snuggles up against my legs when the storm rumbles outside.

At 6 p.m. sharp, I take her for a walk as I continue my day's study—notebook in my left hand, leash in my right. The same hour-long itinerary, every day, never deviating. The seasons pass before my eyes as I stroll along. I watch the foliage and farm fields slowly metamorphose. Patches of damp earth gradually give way to dense rows of corn, restricting my field of vision. The palette of colors offered by the sky is reinvented every day.

These walks are a way for me to keep active, but also to shorten the last hour before dinner. The four 0% yogurts I consume during the day aren't enough to soothe me until evening. My body weakens as 7 p.m. approaches. My face tightens, my jaw clenches, the slightest annoyance irritates me. My whole mind is suspended in anticipation of this meal.

*

The more time I spend alone, the more noise disturbs me. I'm gradually getting used to wearing earplugs all the time. The slightest sound pierces and irritates me. My whole body tenses up at every creak, every breath, every vibration. The hardest part is hearing people eat, chew, swallow and swallow. All the sounds that come from the mouth disgust me. *How can you make so much noise drinking soup or a simple cup of coffee? The most despicable sound is that of raw carrots taking forever to swallow, or that of Alaia chewing her kibble.*

Wounds are forming in my ears from wearing earplugs day and night. Despite these slight lesions, I persist in protecting myself from the sounds around me. When the earplugs aren't enough, I press my hands against my ears. Even silence has become unbearable.

*

At the end of the year, I was taking the brevet as an independent candidate at a state secondary school. Suddenly, I find myself surrounded by young people my own age. Their gestures and topics of discussion seem strange and unfamiliar. I no longer try to fit in with their groups by any means. *The Voice* protects me. *They're not interesting anyway.*

I'm overwhelmed by stress as each test approaches. I'm afraid of failing, of not measuring up. *The Voice* repeats the same phrases over and over in my head. *Show them that you don't need teachers to succeed. Now is the time to give it your all. If you fail, you'll blame yourself for the rest of your life.*

The math test takes place on a particularly hot Friday. Drops of sweat bead on my forehead. I struggle to remember some of the formulas I've learned over the year. Anxiety rises in my chest. *You see, you should have studied more.*

Despite a few scares, I get the "Très bien" mention I've been longing for. *The Voice* applauds me. When I find out the results, I rejoice for a few moments, then *She* recommends that I look at next year's program.

During the summer following the brevet, we spend time with my grandparents in Normandy, then with my maternal grandmother in the Spanish Basque Country. To appear normal, I try to fit in at family meals—with my earplugs and Asian chopsticks.

Unfortunately, it's hard for me to cope, and to follow the flow of the meal with my distinct diet. I'm sometimes ashamed of the foods *The Voice* allows me to eat, and the order in which I eat them. So I lock myself in a separate room and eat while reading books or writing.

Luckily, my paternal grandparents are extremely sympathetic to my behavior. They experienced war in their youth. A bomb fell on my grandfather's house when he was fourteen, killing several of his sisters and his mother. Despite their very difficult backgrounds, my grandparents don't judge my problems, which might seem trivial to them.

For her part, my Basque grandmother goes to discussion groups for relatives of people with eating disorders.

I'm grateful for what they do for me.

One of my biggest regrets from those years of anorexia was how mean I was to both my grandmothers and my mother. I was distraught and took my anger out on the most benevolent people around me—without any apparent logic or reason. I still can't explain why today.

I apologize to them, and thank them for all the love they've shown me since I was born.

*

The eve of the start of the new academic year. I meticulously fold the clothes I'll be wearing on my first day at school—a navy blue top with white embroidery, and a cream-colored jacket. My things have to be in perfect order. *Otherwise, your first day won't go perfectly.* I line up my favorite pens in my pencil case and stow my binder in my new faux-leather bag.

Even though I'm sure I'll miss the CNED at first, I'm excited about joining this high school with its renowned art option. I hope to meet people who are just as fascinated by the arts as I am. It's said that high school represents "the beautiful years", that teenagers mature at this stage of life. So I'm already imagining myself surrounded by new friends and, why not, my first boyfriend. My future seems very clear: next year, I'll be going into the "L" (literary) stream.

Unfortunately, on the eve of the new school year, while I was shopping with my father, my little brother, Unai, called us in a panic: "It's raining in the house!"

We left the supermarket in a hurry and made our way back to the car in the pouring rain. Back at the house, we discover that large streams of water are seeping through the ceiling and dripping onto the tiles, gradually flooding the first floor. I rush to my room and see that water is leaking all over the things I've packed for the new school year. *The Voice* tenses up at the sight of my new bag soaked in dirty water, my school supplies damp and my clothes soaked. *Back to school is going to be a disaster.*

*

I've had a pretty good start to the new school year, and I'm trying to get used to this new daily routine that's still putting me to the test. Every morning at 6:30, I get into the car with my father, whose workplace is close to my high school. On the road, we listen to music and podcasts, while I enjoy an oat bran porridge—the 0% yoghurts aren't enough to stop my stomach rumbling during class, a situation that makes me very uncomfortable. As we drive along, the sun rises and the sky takes on pink and orange hues. The program *Lettres à Élodie* (on Radio Nova) accompanies us for a few precious minutes. I admire this woman who expresses herself with great delicacy and poetry. As we approach the city center, my stomach tightens. I'd like to stay in the car with my father, in the warmth, away from stress and social interaction. Unfortunately, we have to separate until midday, when I meet him for lunch in the car on rainy days, or on a bench overlooking the Pyrenees on sunny days. My mother alternates with my father, making special trips to the city center so as not to leave me alone during the long lunch break. We meet in a park and watch the groups of strollers, imagining their lives and occupations. I'm particularly fond of this park as it has a Japanese garden, which my mother and I contemplate at length, marvelling at every detail. My mother and I share the same vision of what surrounds us, the same sensitivity to color and art. When she's by my side, I feel I'm no longer alone in my world. I could stay with my parents for hours, but unfortunately, it's inevitably time to go back to school.

Little by little, I'm forging links with my new classmates. Unfortunately, I still find it difficult to juggle my food obsessions, my academic perfectionism and contact with my teachers. Despite meeting new people and developing feelings for a boy, my mind is always somewhere else. I resisted for a month and a half—until the All Saints' vacation—and then disappeared again. Once again, I miss the CNED, my method of working, my food and my creative time slots.

Back to solitude, I cry every night before going to bed and fall back into a manic daily routine, lulled by the sound of *The Voice.*

*

Early 2016. A boy sends me a message on Facebook. We chat for a while. At first, I'm bored by these discussions, which feel like they're stealing my time. But as the days go by, I get hooked and go back. *The Voice* fades a little, I want to know more about him. After a few weeks, he insists on meeting me. *She* agrees, on condition that the meeting is short, so that I can work in the evenings. *You absolutely have to pass this year.* After our first meeting, we got together.

He's my first boyfriend. We share a few light moments with his entourage, on the eve of my 16th birthday. He introduces me to his family, with whom I get on very well. This relationship upsets my meticulous organization—meal times, my work and sports schedule—but it brings me a little happiness all the same. At his side, I escape from the CNED and experience the life of a normal teenager.

Unfortunately, our story ends after a month and a half. He left me for another girl, whose body was more formed than mine. This news saddens me enormously. A week before we broke up, he confided in me that one of his friends had said to him:

"What are you doing with her? You won't do anything with her."

This remark made me lose even more confidence in myself and my body.

The day after we broke up, I boarded a train for Paris, tears welling up in my eyes. My mother is by my side. We set off together to visit the art schools that interest me. I want to do the open house early, two years before my final year, to make sure I'm on track.

First, we visit the Gobelins school, which specializes in animation. As soon as we step into the corridors, I feel the tension, the atmosphere of hard work, competition and elitism. Computers are lined up with military precision. Near certain workstations, individual boards are covered with perfect drawings—confident strokes, characters worked in unique, mastered styles. The standard is very high. I can already see that I won't be able to get into this school.

Next, we headed for the École Estienne, specializing in book arts—bookbinding, illustration, engraving. The school's exterior instantly soothes me; it's an old building with orange bricks, bordered by a verdant park. Overhead, swarms of crows flit and caw in chorus. The establishment exudes an atmosphere worthy of a *Harry Potter* film. A mixture of mystery, tradition and magic emanates from every corner.

The school's interior reflects its exterior. Warm, enchanted, steeped in history. A girl with curly brown hair introduces us to her training. The way she expresses herself and her description of the school make me dream. She seems happy here, and I understand her. A new goal is born in me, almost instantly: I'm going to work hard for two years to get into this place, and do my utmost to become a children's book illustrator in the future.

*

The year of general secondary school is validated. *But the hardest part is yet to come, The Voice* keeps telling me.

During the summer vacations, our little dog Alaia dies in the middle of a hike, following the bite of a snake. We hold her in our arms to comfort her. Her frozen, wide-open eyes reflect the blue sky and clouds. It's the first time I've seen death for real. Grieving is going to be difficult; Alaia had been a light, joyful presence in our family since I left hospital.

Two months later, we decided to adopt a new dog called "Aizpa"—which means sister in Basque. Like Alaia, she's a greyhound crossbreed, but taller, with a light coat and strong muscles.

One night, as we were taking her for a walk on the beach, Aizpa ran very quickly in my direction and slammed into me, brutally sweeping across my lower body. The shock was so violent that the sea turned in my eyes. The two bitches I've known are much stronger than I am.

From now on, it's Aizpa who looks after me when I'm home alone.

*

I start my first year of secondary school. This time, I'm not trying to get into a new school. The next two years will be spent at the CNED.

The Voice doesn't let me go. I make no effort to counter it and live in total symbiosis with *Her*. I still haven't sat down during working hours since last year. My weight fluctuates between 44 and 46 kg. *She* tolerates that I consume 1,750 calories a day, not one more. This allows me to maintain just the right weight, where I don't lose too much hair or feel unwell. I'm nearly 17 and haven't had my period for four years. Sometimes I'm afraid I've become sterile. So I intensify my evening prayers, which I address to my own god: *Please let me get my period back while maintaining this weight. Please let me get my period back while maintaining this weight. Please let me get my period back while maintaining this weight.*

Everything must be done in 3's or 9's. *The Voice* likes these numbers, which *She* considers *harmonious, logical and reassuring.*

My daily routine is so repetitive that I sometimes lose track of the days. Like last year, I work from Monday to Sunday, as well as during school vacations. *You've got nothing more important to do than get on with your revisions. The first exams are coming up.*

I do the same physical exercises every day. My exercise routine has evolved since my first break-up, and I'm trying to make certain parts of my body more "feminine" by building up muscle. My ex-boyfriend had advised me to follow the routines of athletic women, with perfectly trimmed bodies, who share their workouts on Instagram. So I set about it, every evening, in the hope of shaping a figure more in line with today's standards.

Every evening, at 6 p.m., I take the same walk with my dog. In the middle of this walk, there's a place I particularly like. It's a path that winds through a green tunnel. This canopy is formed by the tops of tall trees, whose branches filter the daylight and deposit numerous golden spots on the ground. The sound atmosphere is ideal, peaceful. Here, I sometimes manage to remove my earplugs. The silence is only interrupted by the crystalline song of small birds. I often think that, if I were to die anywhere, it would be here.

There's another place that gives me that effect. It's a hilly plain close to my parents' house, where a horse and some sheep graze peacefully. The grass here seems soft, almost velvety. A tree with a slightly curved trunk stands on the left half of the plain. Its silhouette stands out perfectly against the majestic background: the Pyrenees mountain range, brushed by long pink clouds. The field slopes gently down to a deep, dark forest. This forest sometimes strangely attracts me.

Some nights, I imagine myself climbing over the low wall that borders this plain and crossing all the way down—a rope tied to my belt, a cold knife stuck in my back pocket. The forest looms before me, still and silent. I sit on the ground, on the damp leaves, leaning against a tree. I let myself die there, relieving myself of the weight of the days and my powerlessness in the face of *The Voice*.

I'm currently studying this poem by Arthur Rimbaud, which I particularly like and which evokes this feeling: *Le Dormeur du Val*. Here's an extract:

Un soldat jeune, bouche ouverte, tête nue,
Et la nuque baignant dans le frais cresson bleu,
Dort ; il est étendu dans l'herbe, sous la nue,
Pâle dans son lit vert où la lumière pleut.

Les pieds dans les glaïeuls, il dort. Souriant comme
Sourirait un enfant malade, il fait un somme :
Nature, berce-le chaudement : il a froid.[4]

*

During my junior year, I see a new shrink: Monsieur Labernier. It was the first time I'd discussed anorexia with a man, after four years of being treated by women. His approach is interesting, more neutral and distant than what I've experienced in the past. Since Mr. Labernier is the exact opposite of me—a man in his sixties—I feel comfortable talking to him freely, without fear of judgment.

---

4. *A young soldier, mouth open, head bare,*
And neck bathed in fresh blue watercress,
Sleeps; he lies in the grass, beneath the nude,
Pale in his green bed where the light rains.

With his feet in the gladioli, he sleeps. Smiling as
A sick child would smile, he snoozes:
Nature, rock him warm: he's cold.

I regularly confide in him the dark thoughts that haunt me and my fears about the future:

"I'm constantly thinking about death. I feel as if my brain is 'broken,' that there's no way out, no way back."

He looks at me attentively and lets me continue:

"For example, since I know the calories of every food, I don't think I'll ever be able to eat freely again".

One day, at the beginning of winter, when my sadness is particularly pronounced and my weight has dropped slightly, Monsieur Labernier tells me of his concern. He tells me about a center specializing in eating disorders. The very mention of this subject terrifies me. I pull myself together.

To make myself feel less alone in the suffering associated with anorexia nervosa, I sometimes read testimonial books. I'm fascinated by the similarity of the writings, symptoms and reflections. My parents read them too. I hope it will help them to understand my behaviour a little better.

In the course of my reading, I've noticed that many people with anorexia nervosa go through a bulimic phase before leaving the illness. This lack of control still shocks me. It'll never happen to you if you listen to me, don't worry.

*

End of Première L and first steps towards the bac. I'm taking several tests at a public school: written and oral French, written sciences and the TPE (travaux personnels encadrés). For normal high school students, the TPE is group work, but for those enrolled at the CNED, it's individual work. The principle of the TPE is to choose a personal theme around a notion on the syllabus. The final stage is an oral presentation to a jury, accompanied by a written dossier. I'm working on a theme I'm passionate about: "The influence of Japanese culture on Hayao Miyazaki's films".

For an entire term, I prepare a fictitious travel diary—of someone who has traveled to Japan—complete with sketches and anecdotes, which I present at the oral exam. I'm really enjoying writing the dossier, which links the arts, legends, beliefs and customs of Japan to the work of Hayao Miyazaki. Japanese culture is fascinating.

This project calms my year down a little, allowing me to travel through documentation and thought. It also helps me to get away from dark thoughts.

One day, I'll dream of exploring the Japanese countryside by bike and train. Like in *My Neighbor Totoro* or *Spirited Away*.

*

The summer vacations are finally here. I've received my marks for my first baccalaureate exams, which are promising for next year's coveted "Très bien".

I love summer vacation, because it's the only time of year when *The Voice* lets me rest a little. *You still need to keep yourself busy in a "useful" way, by reading quality books, for example.*

Whenever possible, I go to my village library, run by Rose-Marie—a wonderful woman who used to read us stories when we were at school. Her voice is soft and full of magic. Even the most restless among us would keep quiet to listen to her. She has a gift for bringing stories to life.

Rose-Marie watched me grow up, then gradually sink into emaciation and loneliness. She followed me every step of the way, with respect and modesty. Not a single indiscreet question, not a passing glance. She never judged me when I borrowed recipe books in my early teens, when I was very thin and obviously not cooking for myself. Last year, when I was browsing the children's section to learn about the work of the great children's illustrators, she would discreetly approach me and take the time to recommend authors and illustrators I might like.

Most of our conversations take place at the end of the visit, while she scans the books I'm borrowing. These simple conversations forge a link between each week. Today, she recommended Alessandro Baricco's *Silk*. A wonderful novel, an invitation to travel.

I savor every page, hoping one day to escape too.

Sometimes, during the summer, I get a twinge of sadness when I see young people my age partying, having fun with friends, experiencing their first love stories. The same feeling comes over me on New Year's Eve, when my brothers leave home to join their friends. As I drift off to sleep, tears keep rolling down my cheeks. I feel the weight of years spent under the domination of *The Voice*.

My father played me a song by London Grammar, whose lyrics resonate with me:

"Maybe I'm wasting my young years/Don't you know that it's only fear?/I wouldn't worry, you have all your life".

Here's the translation:

"Maybe I'm wasting my young years/Don't you know that it's only fear?/I wouldn't worry, you have all your life ahead of you".

*

I start my final year of high school, the decisive year for the baccalaureate. *The Voice* imposes an increasingly draconian pace on my life. *You have to pass with honors and get into the École Estienne, all while keeping your weight at 45 kg.*

There's not a minute to be lost for *futile hobbies*. The only moments of respite I allow myself must be associated with work: the series I watch after midnight are in English, to practice my listening comprehension. I explore and dissect every notion on the syllabus for days on end. I spend hours making revision sheets on small-square A4 sheets, which I fill with meticulously written texts and colorful diagrams. Everything has to be clear, legible and fun. If I cross out even one word, *The Voice* orders me to start again. I always use the same type of blue pen, with a fine, precise point that never stains the paper. Each revision sheet is filed in a binder dedicated to its subject. I have to give it my all, it's the final sprint.

At the same time as this intensive work, I stop playing basketball. The sport is too time-consuming and I feel the need to distance myself from certain people who remind me too much of my past. To maintain a semblance of social contact, I join a fencing club, where I already feel a little better. My slow reactions mean that I don't excel in this sport either.

In the middle of the year, I put together a portfolio to apply to the École Estienne. To ensure that the final file is perfect, I scrutinize and check each image twenty times, reread and correct each description, and test several formulations for each sentence. There are over five hundred applications for each course, of which eighty are called for oral examinations and only twelve are selected per class. I'm afraid I won't get past the first stage. To maximize my chances of getting into the school, I applied for several courses: Animation, Illustration, Engraving.

Fortunately, a few weeks later, I learned that I'd been invited to the selection interviews in Paris for all three courses. Each specialty is the promise of a dream, even if I have a preference for the Animation and Illustration sections. Engraving is more alien to me. The only thing that links me to this discipline is the fact that my mother practiced it at the Beaux-Arts when she was my age.

A few weeks later, it's time to leave for the interviews in Paris. I ask my mother if we can fly there, as I've never flown before in my life. The idea of flying over the clouds fascinates and attracts me. I wonder what it's like up there.

At the airport, the excitement of departure mixes with unexpected anxiety. The controllers tell me that you can't take yoghurt in your cabin baggage. For the past three years, *The Voice* has only allowed me one brand of yogurt, at

43 calories each. *If you leave them here, you'll be destabilized and fail the interview. Besides, tomorrow's a bank holiday, so you won't be able to buy any on the spot.* I'm ashamed of that moment when the stress and the stakes of the interview were so high that I begged my mother to pay for a hold bag to take the yoghurts to Paris.

The day before the interviews, I'm overwhelmed by stress. I feel like my life is on the line. My mother tries to soothe me as best she can, but I can't help being tense and unpleasant. *The Voice* has high hopes for this school. *The interview has to go perfectly. Be careful how you express yourself, and don't forget all the descriptions you've memorized.* I fall asleep with difficulty, at my mother's side, in a small hotel room nestled in the 13th arrondissement.

The next morning, I grab my large drawing case and head for the École Estienne. In the corridors, I'm petrified. Other candidates wait beside me. *They're definitely better than you.*

Unfortunately, the interviews don't go as well as I'd hoped. I do my best to present my work, but the jury in front of me is intransigent.

"You're from the CNED, aren't you? You know that the École Estienne is very demanding."

"Yes, but it's my dream."

"You mustn't confuse dreams with reality."

I leave the interview in tears, convinced that I'll never get into my dream school. To help me come to my senses, my mother leads me to a bench near the school, where we sit down. The plane tree leaves wave above us. It's a magical place.

*

A month later, I took my baccalauréat littéraire exams. The stress had been so intense the week before that I sometimes banged my head against the window panes in my bedroom—to punish myself for not having assimilated enough knowledge. *You'll never make it.* To appease *The Voice,* I continue to work tirelessly, copying down every definition of a concept I don't know perfectly, delving into every subject, studying the annals of previous years' exams. One evening, I break down and my mother tries to calm me down. Together we reread all the binders of revision sheets I'd created for myself over the year. I ask her to ask me practice questions.

My father, too, gives me the strength to get through the home stretch. He drives me to the exams every morning. We chat and listen to music on the way, to lighten the mood. I breathe deeply before each test, fear in my stomach.

The week goes by with difficulty. Each exam represents the culmination of years of solitude and hard work. I *have to* pass everything.

Some time later, I open the online results service and discover that I've passed my bac with distinction. A tear of happiness rolls down my cheek—it's never happened to me before. I'm overcome by a feeling of joy and relief. *The Voice* embraces me and says:

"See, I told you, it was worth the pain."

*

To get into the École Estienne, you need to have an impeccable academic record: excellent grades, exemplary behavior and a high school diploma. So there's only one step left before I know the turning point for the year ahead: the results of the selection interviews.

A few days after the baccalauréat results, I discover that the selection lists for the École Estienne have been published. I shut myself away in my room, sitting on a carpet, my phone clutched in my trembling hands. I was accepted for engraving—but on the waiting list—and rejected for animation and illustration. *A failure.* The announcement is painful, difficult to digest. I collapse once more, curled up on my bedroom floor. After a while, I get up again, then go for a walk with my dog, crying, on the plain surrounding my village's water tower. *The Voice* is upset. *This isn't what you had planned. She* reminds me over and over.

After two days, fortunately, hope returns. My application moves up the waiting list. I become eligible for the engraving program. The news fills me with joy. I clicked on the "Confirm my final choice" button without hesitation.

In two months' time, I'll be off to Paris.

Paris

August 2018, age 18

After four and a half years of distance learning, recluse in my childhood village, I'm off to my dream school in Paris. This step is a straightforward transition—between the silence of my village and the hustle and bustle of the capital, between CNED courses and a return to society. This change may seem risky, but I prefer it that way. Sometimes, it's better to turn the page frankly. This new beginning is a source of hope. A chapter opens. A new life begins.

After hours of searching on rental websites, I find a superb apartment in the 6th arrondissement. A 12 m^2 maid's room, nestled on the 4th floor of a Haussmann building—with a view of the Eiffel Tower. My parents let me live this daydream. We drove across France, our trunks loaded with bags overflowing with clothes, interior decorations and art supplies. Together, we set up this pretty cocoon, my very first home. We laugh happily as we set up, excited to see this dream come true.

Then it's time to leave. Night falls softly over Paris. From my bedroom window, I watch my parents return to the car and wave at them—the same gesture we used to make with my father in hospital. They smile at me before walking away. I hope to show them that I can do it this time.

As the car disappears around the corner, a deep silence fills the room. The noise of the city reaches me softly: the honking and coming and going of cars and buses, the laughter of customers in the bar downstairs, my neighbor's door slamming. All these sounds are totally foreign to me. I close the window. For the first time, I'm truly alone. *The Voice* is by my side, but I soon realize that his presence is no match for the company of those closest to me. I already miss my parents. Fortunately, they call me after ten minutes:

"It was hard, those goodbyes!"

*

First morning alone in Paris, I race down the stairs of my dream building, steeped in the magic of a bygone century, then head for the Luxembourg Gardens, which are close to my home.

I listen to "Il est cinq heures... Paris... s'éveille..." (It's five o'clock... Paris... wakes up...) on my headphones as I make my way through the streets of 6th arrondissement of Paris. I'm amazed by the sculpted facades, moldings and refined lampposts, by the brightness of the flowers hanging from the balconies and by the charm of the Parisian cafés. I feel like I've stepped back in time, plunged into an era when the streets were alive with artists and poets. I sit down on one of the wrought-iron chairs in the Luxembourg Gardens and savor the end of the book I was reading this summer, lulled by the elegant, poetic atmosphere of this park.

On the way back, I stop at a local bakery to buy a loaf of raisin bread. I ask the saleswoman to serve me one in particular—plump and not overcooked. For some time now, *The Voice* has allowed me this pleasure once a week. *As long as I photograph the raisin bread and record on a chart: its weight to the nearest gram, its price, the name of the bakery it came from, and the date and exact weight I weighed the week I ate it. To make sure it doesn't cause any damage.* The table and the photographs of the raisin loaves are stored in a special folder on my hard disk. *The Voice* is reassured by the graphic and mysterious shape of this pastry. For my part, I revel in the soft texture of the brioche dough (which I prefer to puff pastry), the sweetness of the custard and the sumptuous aroma of rum-soaked raisins. I've been dreaming of tasting a viennoiserie like this for six years. This rediscovery is exceptional, each bite an explosion of flavors, reminding me of the carefree greed of childhood.

I'm only entitled to this reward when my sports routine is complete and all the data on the raisin bread is carefully recorded. *When it's time to eat, it must also be warmed up in the microwave, to develop its aromas, and eaten from the outside in. Never any other way.* Since this new habit is supervised by *The Voice,* and doesn't affect my 45 kg, I'm able to enjoy myself without feeling guilty.

The Voice even invites me to eat more and more spiral-shaped foods.

The day before school starts, I discover that my mini-fridge isn't working. The forty 0% yogurts I've stocked in there are changing texture, making my mealtime experience worse. *You're wasting calories eating bad food. Lukewarm, runny yoghurts.* I'm going to have to find a solution quickly. I call my landlady, who promises to deliver a small fridge at the end of the week. In the meantime, I have no choice but to eat liquid yoghurt.

*

I start my first year at the École Estienne. I touch my dream with my fingertips. In the metro, heading for the Place d'Italie, I watch the passengers carefully: an old man with an accordion, a lonely child, a man in a suit, a woman immersed in her book, a couple of tourists. I'm amazed by this diversity, this mix of intermingling lives. The metro doors open and my heart races. I grab the straps of my backpack and plunge into the stream of passers-by moving through the many corridors of the Place d'Italie metro station. I love being part of this compact, hurried crowd. When I realize how many people there are around me, my problems seem insignificant.

As I emerge from the metro, a fresh breeze caresses my face. It's colder than in the South at this time of year. After a few minutes' walk, I catch sight of the orange facade of the École Estienne, visible through the rows of plane trees. I take a deep breath, then enter the courtyard where I went with my mother two years ago for the open house, and a few months ago for the selection interviews. I think hard about her.

I'm relieved when I realize that the people in my class are very kind and open-minded. From our very first exchanges, I'm impressed by their elocution, their curiosity and their ease in talking about art. I discover that here, my favorite animated film director, Hayao Miyazaki, is a household name. I can finally talk about *Castle in the Sky* or *Ponyo on the Cliff* with young people my own age. The students' political ideas are also very similar to my own. I'm in an extraordinary bubble, an enchanted manor house right in the center of Paris. Conversations and ideas flow. I feel at home for the first time.

The Voice is ecstatic; *she*'d never known a place that brought together so many captivating people.

"You are France's elite!" proclaims the school's principal in the amphitheater.

A classmate whispers to me:

"Maybe that's a bit excessive."

The school's high standards are quickly apparent. The class hours are dense and the artistic projects to be carried out at the same time very substantial. I struggled to keep up with the pace of work from the very first week. I was intimidated by the level of my classmates' drawing and the demands of the teachers.

On our first class outing—sketching in the Parc de la Villette—one of my teachers put her head over my shoulder, leaned towards my sketchbook and said:

"It's dead what you're doing... Try to let go. It lacks plasticity".

Plasticity? I don't even know that word... That evening, when I got back to my little room, I collapsed in bed, crying. These first few days of classes have taken their toll on me. Getting used to this new rhythm of life, to the workings of such a big city, meeting so many people, learning how to manage my apartment, eating late at night when I get home from class, finding out that all my classmates are brilliant and that I don't understand the teachers' demands. It's a lot. *Maybe you're just not up to it. Accept that, from now on, you'll be one of the bottom of the class.*

My tears soak the water cushion, and I have to turn it regularly to let it dry a little.

The first worries of adult life are hard to deal with. My new mini-fridge arrives this Friday lunchtime, and I take the metro back and forth during my break to collect it. As I arrive at the foot of the building, I see the delivery man dropping a huge parcel on the first floor.

"Could you help me get it upstairs? I don't have much arm strength... And I live alone."

The deliveryman looks at me furtively, then says:

"No. I'm sorry. Sorry, I don't have the time."

Once again, this innocuous situation puts my nerves to the test. I'm afraid I'll be late for my afternoon class in the first week back, and that my teacher won't take kindly to me.

I take a deep breath and lean against the cardboard to push it, millimetre by millimetre, to the elevator. My head spins with every impulse. The last little step makes it even harder. I break down. My eyes well up with tears. I sit on the floor and cry, alone, in the lobby of my building. After a few minutes, I pull myself together and try to sheathe the tiny muscles in my arms. Finally, I tip the box over the small step and pull it towards me in the elevator. Unfortunately, when I reach the top floor, I realize I'm stuck behind the box. I don't have enough clearance to push it and I don't have enough space to get out. How could I not have thought of this before? I'm such a fool... More tears roll down my cheeks. Finally, I climb over the box as best I can to get out of the cabin. Then I pull the parcel out, leaning back, with the strength of my little arms. It seemed an insurmountable daily ordeal.

That evening, I called my parents and had a long talk with my mother—for about three hours. She always had the words to reassure me.

*

Second week of school. I go to the school nurse's office to inform her of my situation, so that I'll have someone to turn to, on the spot, in case of a problem. She's a nice person, but her character is a bit strange. She looks at me with round eyes and her head tilted slightly to one side when I speak to her. After a few moments, she says to me:

"Your parents are irresponsible for letting you come to Paris on your own".

She pauses, then continues:

"After years of being out of school and not quite out of anorexia, it's a very risky gamble".

I take a breath and calmly explain that my parents are fully aware of the situation. No decision was taken lightly. And I had to try to spread my wings one day.

Fortunately, as the weeks went by, I gradually managed to open up to several of my classmates. Little by little, trust began to grow, and I discovered their respective backgrounds and confided in them snippets of my past, particularly those long years of social isolation. I sometimes fear that they'll judge me if I don't have the right codes for an exchange, or when I need to get away from the group, to rest a little and find *The Voice* again. I fear that this need for solitude will be interpreted as coldness. But to my great surprise, my comrades don't judge me. They welcome me as I am, with patience, gentleness and kindness. I'm amazed by their sensitivity and maturity, and they change the way I look at young people my own age.

Every weekend, the people in my class get together for parties and activities such as concerts and museum visits. Unfortunately, I can't join them. *The Voice is* always calling out to me, so I spend hours in the silence of my apartment with *Her.* Sometimes we go out together, walking briskly through the streets of Paris, in search of the weekly pain aux raisins. *It has to be ideal, the experience has to be exhilarating. Otherwise, it would be dramatic.*

The loneliness I'm experiencing here is much heavier than that of my years at CNED, when I used to meet up with my brothers and parents in the evenings. The most difficult time is the weekend, when I'm totally alone for almost 48 hours.

To make up for this void, I spend my Saturdays doing the week's shopping. The brand of 0% yoghurt tolerated by *The Voice* is to be found in a supermarket about twenty minutes from my home, by bus. I spend about an hour there, taking care to select each item correctly, checking the composition of each food. The slightest mistake could trigger an avalanche of reproaches from *The Voice*. *How could you confuse a bottle of Cherry Coke with a bottle of Coke Zero? You're really absent-minded. For your trouble, you'll eat less tonight.*

When transport is late, errands can take me up to half a day. It happened to me once, at the beginning of winter, that the bus didn't come once I'd finished my shopping. I waited for about thirty minutes, huddled in the windy bus shelter, and then resigned myself to carrying the forty yoghurts and the rest of my groceries home on foot, by force of arms. The further I walked, the more my arms trembled, tetanized by cold and fatigue. It wasn't long before my hands were aching from the handles of my shopping bags. The more time passed, the more the cold crept into the sleeves of my jacket, sliding down my spine and across my stomach. Such was my exhaustion and weariness that I began to cry. Passers-by on the street would furtively cross my gaze, looking questioningly at me. I moved very slowly and stopped regularly, putting the bags at my feet, short of breath, legs wobbling. In the middle of a street that seemed endless, snowflakes fell on my face, then on my hands, wetting my clothes and the handles of my bags. This made the journey all the harder.

After long minutes of walking, I took refuge in my bed, shaking with fatigue. Why is *The Voice forcing* me to shop so far away when I have a supermarket just down the road?

*

Despite the difficulties of everyday life, I'm starting to get into the rhythm of Parisian life. I'm constantly listening to music in the metro and on the street. The atmosphere of this city fascinates me, and perfectly matches the poetry, elegance and melancholy that *The Voice* particularly appreciates.

In the evenings, before going to bed, I watch the Eiffel Tower sparkle from my rounded bedroom window, a steaming cup of tea in hand. My parents support me and keep me company on the phone every day. I feel more stable and serene as the weeks go by. I have the feeling that, this time, I'm going to stand my ground and not go back to work at home.

*

Late Friday afternoon, I'm in a printmaking class. Sitting in front of the printing plate I've been working on for days, my fingers are trembling and my shoulders are tense. *Every line you engrave is twisted. Apply yourself.* The perfectionism that *The Voice* inflicts on me on this exercise is a real pain. After several mistakes, I put down my work tool and look out the window facing my desk. My mind wanders as I observe the night landscape. I think of my parents, whom I miss terribly. I long for the years wasted by anorexia, all the time when *She* hogged my parents' attention, stealing it from my brothers. Guilt gnaws at me. I'm afraid I've exhausted my parents and deprived my brothers of lightness. A wave of sadness washes over me, tears rolling down my cheeks.

Suddenly, I hear a student's voice coming from the staircase leading to the workshop. The sound spreads through the room. I glance back to see a tall young man enjoying himself with a friend. I remember seeing him once in the schoolyard. But I didn't think he was in the engraving speciality, in a different grade from me. I noticed that his haircut had changed. When I first met him, he was wearing dreadlocks, tied back. Now, his hair is short and curly.

I pull myself together and get on with my work. Then, a few moments later, I feel a presence at my back.

"Can anyone lend me a magazine?"

I turn around and shyly hand it to him. Then he says, smiling:

"Thank you very much!"

His eyes are an intense, shiny black—like marbles. A moustache turned up at the sides of his mouth emphasizes his smile. He disappears upstairs, waddling happily.

I turn to my friend and whisper:

"Shame, I was crying."

The next day, as I walk through the school hall with a friend, I catch a glimpse of her silhouette in the distance. I look away slightly, thinking he won't recognize me. But he smiles and greets me with a wave, to which I respond awkwardly.

A few days later, at the school Christmas market, I make it my mission to discover his first name on the prints he's selling. I wander down the aisles, head bowed, and catch a glimpse of him in the distance. He's leaning against a wall, arms folded, laughing with a friend from his class. I shyly approach his stand and catch a glimpse of the name: Thomas.

I ask a friend who knows some of the upper-level students, and discover that he's a tattoo artist as well as a student.

*

The Christmas vacations are finally here. I happily head down south, relieved to get away from the hustle and bustle of Paris. The train winds its way through rows of pine trees. These landscapes remind me of my childhood weekends, when we'd go away in a truck for just a few nights, and it instantly soothes me. I'm so happy to be back with my loved ones. Although I haven't shared Christmas meals with them for five years, I still enjoy the warmth of the festive season. The twinkling lights, the scent of simmering dishes and the glitter of gift wrap remind me of the carefree days of childhood. The magic of Christmas is still with me. I try to put on a brave face during the aperitif and gift-giving, but end up isolating myself in my room. My Christmas menu is identical to the one I've eaten every evening for so many years. Ham, steamed vegetables and yoghurt, which I eat while reading. I sit alone with *The Voice*, who also enjoys the nostalgia of Christmas, and all the events connected with food.

Tonight, I sleep in my childhood bedroom. Before going to bed, I get up to go to the bathroom. On the way, my toe strikes a small object on the floor. I struggle to reach the bathroom and discover that my foot is bleeding slightly. Then, suddenly, a feeling of emptiness invades my head. Like almost six years ago, in hospital, I collapse to the floor. My head hits the edge of the shower with a thud. My nose and temples burst open in shock.

I'm awakened by the cries of a child, as on my previous occasions of discomfort, before realizing that these complaints belong to me.

I lie on the cold tiles, unable to move. After a few minutes, I reach for the sink and discover my reflection in the mirror. The top of my nose is gouged. My face is pale, sunken with fatigue and smeared with blood.

I feel as if I'm back to my teenage self.

The next morning, I weigh myself and realize that I've lost a little weight since the last vacation.

*

Back to Paris. Despite the tiredness and sadness that never leave me, I love the quiet of my little apartment, where no one makes a sound. I unpack and study for the art history exam we have the next day.

On my way to school, I spot Thomas walking on the same sidewalk as me, but in the opposite direction. I smile shyly at him, then look down. Suddenly, I see his feet blocking my path. I look up, and Thomas jokingly says to me:

"Watch where you're going!"

Thomas is very teasing, which sometimes throws me off balance. Since I'm shy, I don't know where to stand or how to react. One evening, when we were out with the second-year etching students, I had the misfortune to say in front of everyone that I wasn't tactile. A friend had just put her arm around my neck, and the sensation oppressed me. I was laughed at for several hours about it. It didn't really bother me, because I like to be teased. The evening wore on, and then, without warning, Thomas took me in his arms, giggling. I let myself go for a few seconds, then pushed him away with both hands, moaning. A friend of his exclaimed:

"When it's Thomas, though, it's okay apparently!"

The hugging sensation was far from unpleasant, but *The Voice* hates physical contact. *You can see you're not comfortable and you don't know where to put yourself. She doesn'*t like parties either, because they get in the way of my meticulous dinner planning. Besides, I've never drunk alcohol in my life, as *it's a calorific drink. The Voice* believes that *alcohol stupefies human beings*. But I don't mind going out without a drink, I still have a good time with the students at my school.

As the days go by, I feel Thomas' presence taking up more and more space in my head, and *The Voice* doesn't like it.

*

From time to time, I consume the contents of my dinner at breakfast, to free myself up at the end of the day to go to the Friday evenings with the upper-level engravers. *The Voice* doesn't approve of this new organization, and makes me suffer when the evenings are finally cancelled. *You see, you should have listened to me instead of focusing on the boys.* I feel torn between the desire to have adventures with people my own age and the cult of thinness imposed by *The Voice* since I was 12. I have the impression that the disease is irreversible, that I'll suffer from it forever. I'm afraid there's no way out, and that I'll never know another moment of freedom.

One evening, as I lie in bed, my gaze drifts to the kitchen. I watch the knives and pots. I see myself grabbing them, then slitting my wrists, before plunging them into the water.

Exhausted, I call my parents and ask if I can go back to the South of France for a few days to rest. They agreed. The day after my departure, I receive a message from Thomas:

"I noticed you weren't at school today... is everything okay?"

Without thinking too much, I tell him about my journey. He replies that he's touched by what I've told him and suggests I call him that evening. I'm extremely stressed when I pick up the phone, but the call goes well.

The call is barely over when *The Voice* reminds me that it's time to start my daily exercise routine.

On the day I returned to school, while printing engravings in the studio, hands came to rest on my shoulders. *The Voice* immediately tensed up at this physical contact. Fortunately, I soon recognized Thomas' voice:

"Oh la la, that's poor cleaning!"

He was joking. And I replied, still very first-degree:

"It's because my cloth is dirty."

In turn, I approached his desk to leaf through the book he was working on with his friend. As I turned the pages, I pointed out that there was a duplicate. He looked at me for a moment and said, still laughing:

"Great! You've ruined our project".

He smiled at me and stood up. The golden light of the workshop settled on his face. I thought he was handsome. The sound of *The Voice* fades completely when I look at him.

Alongside the relationships that are gradually forming, I continue to work tirelessly at the school. Sometimes, I leave so many sheets of ink and paint on the floor of my room to dry that I can't even put my feet on the floor. I jump from my bed to my little wooden table, to reach the bathroom. In the course of the subjects proposed by the teachers, I discover a passion for Klein's color blue—which I find melancholy, fairylike and *pure*. *The Voice* shares this fascination with me. Every single one of my works has to feature it. This passion for blue becomes obsessive.

I work assiduously to keep up with the pace imposed by school. I spend one sleepless night after another, pencil in hand, listening to the radio, music or podcasts. Being alone in my apartment, I talk out loud to myself. The rhythm of school is exhausting. I break down some days, but this is the first time since middle school that I've managed to stay in one place for so long.

*

Spring is approaching. The magnolias in the school grounds are blooming. One morning, I pass Thomas in the entrance hall. As soon as he sees me, he rolls his eyes and turns back, laughing, before finally turning around to greet me. Since he's wearing shorts, I get my first glimpse of his fully tattooed legs. They're magnificent.

We sit on the grass in the schoolyard and talk at length about the art of tattooing.

I've noticed recently that the girls Thomas dates are more "fleshy" than I am. They all have "womanly" curves. I sometimes find myself envying them, with my childlike body, and I've got it in my head to take on a bit of shape to please Thomas. It's the start of a negotiation between my desires and those of *The Voice.* Unfortunately, I'm no match for *her*. My efforts are in vain. Every time I try to take a step forward, I fall further back, and end up crying in my room at night.

One morning, I look in the mirror and see that my body has become even thinner. Since the first heat of the year, I've been eating nothing but children's popsicles at 40 calories a pop. I eat fifteen a day, for a total of 600 calories. *The Voice* likes Mickey Mouse ice creams, which *are less scary* because they're cute. I fetch them on foot, in the 14th arrondissement, in the sweltering heat of the sun. Every step is difficult, the intensity of the light dazzling me. I nearly faint several times in the street. Then I lock myself in my apartment, the heat and restriction consuming what little fat I have left. I listen to the same music over and over, slumped in bed.

En Léa by Muddy Monk.

June 21, 2019, fête de la musique. I isolate myself in my room, curtains drawn to keep out the heat, resigned to not going out tonight. The air is heavy and dense. I call my parents and have a long talk with them. It's good for me.

Suddenly, I receive an unexpected double call. It's Thomas! He asks me what I'm doing tonight. My heart races, I jump for joy and call my parents to tell them. They're happy for me.

I get ready and we meet at a subway station. I feel very stressed, but Thomas puts me at ease. We meet up with some friends and settle down in a small square in the heart of the Butte-aux-Cailles. The temperature is pleasant on this early summer evening, and there's a joyful, festive atmosphere in the air. Thomas sits on a railing beside me, rocking back and forth, one hand plunged into a packet of potato chips. He offers me some. I take a step back and politely decline. He laughs and asks:

"Why can't you eat chips?"

"I don't know... it scares me. Besides, I'm not hungry."

"OK! So, can I at least invite you for a cocktail, before Guillaume's concert?"

I refuse, too, because I'm still afraid of the calories in alcohol. *The Voice* hates liquid calories, which *She* considers useless because they don't fill you up. Besides, I know the exorbitant prices of cocktails in Paris and would be embarrassed if he spent his money on me. Thomas accompanies me to the Taverne (the name of the bar where the school's engravers meet), as I have to go to the toilet. On my way out, I see him waiting for me, two glasses of Ricard in his hand, a smile on his face. Emotions surge and my eyes well up with tears. *The Voice* falls silent as I look at Thomas. At this very moment, *she*'s no longer my priority. Years of control and suffering fade away. I toast for the first time with an alcoholic glass, and say to Thomas:

"I feel like I'm in a dream..."

"Of course you're in a dream, look at what a hunk you're with!"

We laugh, then dance down the street. The sky is rosy and everything seems light and beautiful.

*

It's the start of summer vacation, and I'm leaving Paris at last. The train pulls away from Montparnasse station, the gray facades giving way to farmland that stretches as far as the eye can see. I'm going to miss Thomas, but I'm happy to be back with my family. My mother welcomes me with her usual kindness. She listens to my new worries about my emotional life, and takes the time to reassure me. I spend hours working at the family dining table. The École Estienne demands a lot of rigor, and we're asked to do a lot of work during the vacations.

My father drives out once a week to buy me a loaf of raisin bread. He leaves it for me on the table before he leaves and writes little notes on the packages, such as "On a qu'une fois vingt ans!"[5] or "Ça va aller! Jtm"[6]. I find these messages very touching and take photos of them every time. Together, we sometimes hike in the Pyrenees, just like when I was little. The dizzying sight of the mountains stretching out in front of me soothes me, as if their immensity stifles my thoughts.

One morning, before setting off on my hike, I manage to eat a more substantial breakfast than usual—a banana and two toasted rolls. My father is proud of me, and informs my mother over the phone. His smile dampens the sound of *The Voice*'s incessant grumbling. During the climb, *The Voice*'s criticisms multiply in my head. For the first time, I try to cope:

"You've completely exceeded the number of calories allowed at breakfast."

"I know... but I need a bit of strength for hiking. Besides, I'd like to have a bit more of a woman's shape, less of a complex about my skinny arms and flat torso."

"You won't feel good in this new body, that's for sure. If you go on like this, you'll ruin all the efforts you've made over the years. You'll end up with other complexes, much more difficult to live with than the ones you have today".

I think hard about Thomas and his cheerful company, and fight every day against *The Voice*. An idea gradually emerges in my head. I set myself the goal of reaching 49 kg, and having Thomas tattoo my hip to engrave this victory in my skin.

I work hard all summer and reach 46.7 kg. The inner dialogues with *The Voice* are more and more frequent. I find

5. You're only twenty once!
6. It'll be okay, I love you!

it hard to interact with those closest to me when *she* criticizes me, and I become bitter and savage with everyone who calls me out.

Don't think Thomas will like you if you get rounder, he might think you're less beautiful. Thinness is your charm.

*

Back to second year. I return to the printmaking studio, nestled under the roofs of the École Estienne. The scents of ink and paper that permeate the place are now familiar to me. I'm delighted to learn that we start the week with a joint class with Thomas.

He sits down on the table next to me and we chat about our summer vacation. At the end of the conversation, I tell him about my weight gain and tattoo project. Thomas looks at me with shining eyes and says, smiling:

"Make it 50 kg!"

He understood that the 50kg barrier seemed psychologically unattainable. *The Voice* takes offence. *49 kg is enough.* But the desire to be tattooed by Thomas and to please him is stronger.

Thomas's temperament is the opposite of *The Voice*'s. He's laughing and sunny. He's laughing, sunny, his movements fluid and relaxed. I was impressed once when I saw him dance at a school party. He seemed in perfect harmony with the music, as if his body knew no constraints. For my part, I stood motionless, a glass of water compressed in my hands.

I used to love to dance when I was little, but since *The Voice* has been tormenting me, I feel as if I'm trapped in a cage too small for me and can't move. My limbs are compressed in a vise.

Throughout the evening, I watched people coming and going from the buffet, helping themselves to drinks and cookies. They all seemed carefree and happy. *The Voice* formally forbade me to go near the table, which was covered in forbidden foods. *You can't eat in front of strangers anyway.*

I suffer during the evenings, but I like going there to meet Thomas.

One day, I say to him:

"I hope you'll get to know me one day with the peach I had when I was a kid".

*

The start of the All Saints' vacation marked a turning point: I managed to put on 2 kg in seven weeks. The weight gain was painful, and I felt as if I'd lost all my bearings. My morale is so low that my psychiatrist prescribes antidepressants. This treatment alleviates my dark thoughts a little and gives me just enough courage to carry on for the rest of the year.

As soon as I return to Paris, I feel that something is changing inside me. *The Voice* sometimes disappears for a while, giving me the impression of being more flexible on certain subjects, only to resurface and criticize me violently. *You'd never have done that a few years ago; you lose control completely.*

Stops at the bakery become more and more frequent. I'm rediscovering foods that my palate has forgotten for almost seven years. Last year, *The Voice* allowed me to eat spiral pastries—such as raisin bread or cinnamon rolls—once a week. As my attraction to novelty gets out of hand, I negotiate with *Her* to eat new foods—such as almond croissants and salty snacks—twice a week. These "pleasure" foods still have to be catalogued, photographed and stored on my hard drive—*to keep everything under control.*

After so many years of starvation, my body is crying out for fatty, floury and sweet foods. I can't fight it anymore. Culinary fantasies mobilize all my thoughts and, unlike a few years ago, I give in to some of my wildest dreams. With each bite, I revel in the buttery notes that melt in my mouth. I rediscover the deliciousness of melted cheese. The scent of oil encrusted in potatoes.

Every week, I plan the two pleasures I'll indulge in the following week. I try to integrate these dizzying desires into my daily routine so as not to fall into a food crisis.

In November 2019, I reach 50 kg. *The Voice* grits its teeth and screams in my head. *You've tipped over the line. You're going back to the way you were. Fat and uncomfortable.* Fortunately, I realize that my parents are proud of this breakthrough. Their reaction comforts me a little. I didn't betray *The Voice* for nothing.

I find it hard to recognize myself in the mirror. New, more "feminine" shapes metamorphose my silhouette, softening the angles of areas of my body that were hollowed out in the past. I don't find these changes so unpleasant to look at, I'm just afraid that the weight gain will never stop.

As agreed, I send a photo of the scale to Thomas.

"Great! When are we setting up that tattoo appointment?"

The Voice steps back and lowers his head, without a sound.

*

November 23, 2019. Thomas creates my very first tattoo. A bouquet of lady's wallflowers, which adapts to the curve of my hip. It's a design he'd done before, which I really liked. I see in this tattoo the symbolism of rediscovered femininity and the beginning of a way out of anorexia. Thomas is an apprentice tattoo artist in Toulouse, but works from time to time in his student room. This is where he arranged for me to get my first tattoo. During the session, the room is bathed in a subdued atmosphere, with music accompanying each creative step. It's a magical, timeless moment.

I really like the result of the tattoo, which allows me to see this area of my body from a different angle.

At the end of the session, in the evening, Thomas invites me to stay for dinner at his and his roommate's, Matteo, who is adorable. *The Voice*, which had been silent since this morning, was directly indignant:

"No! This day has already been hard enough. You need to go home and have your usual dinner."

"But I so want to stay with them... Please, let me enjoy this moment. I haven't allowed myself anything for so many years."

The Voice doesn't answer me. The more the days go by, the more I manage to find arguments to convince her. At the end of some internal debate, *she* finally shuts up.

I can then enjoy the evening and the presence of Thomas, who cooks us pasta with pesto—a fabulous flavor I'd never tasted before. I enjoy the slightly firm texture of the al dente pasta. For dessert, Thomas and Matteo nibble on sour sweets. Caught up in the euphoria of the moment, I allow myself to taste one. Thomas accompanies me, one hand on my shoulder. The pungent sugar coats my palate, an intense pleasure that takes me back to my childhood birthday parties.

"You see, it's done!" says Thomas, winking at me.

Unfortunately, the criticisms of *The Voice* come back very quickly. *Why did you do that? Candy is the worst thing ever. Besides, you didn't know how many calories they contain.* To shut her up, I close my eyes, wrap my arms tightly around Thomas and doze off against him. He's watching *Big Bang Theory* with Matteo. Their laughter soothes me and slowly fades as I fall asleep. I feel so at home with them.

Unfortunately, *The Voice* wakes me up. *What are you still doing here? You've got class tomorrow. And you haven't even studied for the test.* On the way back to the metro, *she*'s talking on a loop in my head. *You could have avoided that candy, it wasn't necessary. Besides, you've been lying on a table all day.*

The next day, I take my courage in hand and confide in Thomas that I have feelings for him. Unfortunately, he explains that he's just come out of a long relationship and needs some time to himself.

I understand, but still cry when I get home that evening.

*

As the days go by, I feel like I'm losing control. The 50 kg mark was supposed to be an insurmountable limit, but my food cravings just won't let up. I can't stop thinking about food all the time. My mouth is salivating at all hours of the day. I stop in front of every bakery I pass, drawn by the scent of warm bread and caramelized sugar. I buy sandwiches or pastries—up to eight at a time.

"Well... that makes a big snack," says the baker.

I gobble them up as I walk along, frantically, without taking the time to chew.

The more the days go by, the more I feel lost, stripped of everything I was. I'd like to divert my attention from these desires that run through me several times a day, but I can't.

In the hope of regaining control and the presence of *The Voice,* I join the gym. Several times a week, I run, cycle and lift weights in an attempt to erase these excesses. I naively watch the gym regulars, as I'm not sure how to use the machines or which exercises to start with. Unfortunately, my body doesn't follow. When I run on the mat, my breath is short, wheezy and irregular. I have the feeling that the sugar rises are clogging my lungs and making my heart race. During each session, I am confronted with my worn and puffy face, in the multiple mirrors that cover the walls of the room.

The Voice is no longer there to guide me. I miss *Her* terribly.

I don't dare go near Thomas since I confided my feelings to him. I feel more alone than ever.

Parisian transport is on strike today, and I've run out of battery on my cell phone. So I wander the streets trying to find my way back to my apartment, trying to get my bearings from the Montparnasse Tower, which looms in the distance. I stop at a kiosk, where I order a mozzarella and tomato sandwich. I swallow it in a few mouthfuls, without even savoring it, mechanically. Then, further on, in a small supermarket, I buy a liter of lemon juice—with pulp—and a box of apple fritters, which I swallow in a quarter of an hour. Tears stream down my face. I press on and stop at one last bakery, where I order four viennoiseries—a chocolate chip ficelle, a coffee éclair, an apple turnover and a spread-filled muffin. I wolf them down one after the other, alternating with sips of lemon juice. The acidity of the juice burns my throat, flaying my stomach. I feel so heavy I can barely walk. I stagger down the street, my heart pounding against my chest.

When I finally arrive home, I kneel down in front of the toilet and slide the handle of a toothbrush down my throat, my hands trembling. I used to criticize people with bulimia... I'm right in the middle of it. I'm trying, but I can't do it. Each attempt exhausts me a little more. After a while, I realize that I can't really make myself vomit. A wave of despair washes over me. I sob, slumped against the cold toilet bowl. My face is wet with tears and saliva. A cry of pain escapes me, I bang my head against the tiles. My knees slide to the floor, my nails dig into my sides. I'd like to pierce my body, rip off all this fat. To find emptiness and *purity*.

Suddenly, a familiar voice emerges from behind my back. *See, I told you to listen to me. You can't even make yourself throw up.* I beg her to stay and help me, but *she* doesn't listen and disappears. I struggle to my feet and look at myself in the mirror. My eyes are red from crying and the skin on my face is pale, marbled with veins and purplish patches from repeated suffocation.

These fits of hyperphagia are multiplying by the day. I'm wasting my parents' money and have no self-esteem. *You're good for nothing.*

One morning, on the way to school, the button on my pants breaks. I pick it up in the middle of the street, ashamed, and go home to change. It's a moment that's hard to live with.

I make an appointment with a psychologist in Paris, to try to regain my footing and curb my compulsions. As I describe the suffering associated with my attacks, he observes me with a distracted air, and ends up advising me:

"All you have to do is drink large quantities of water, that'll block your hunger!"

After a long call with my mother, I decide to leave the École Estienne, abandon my studies and move back to the South of France. The hyperphagia was becoming too violent, and I feared it would get worse indefinitely.

News of my departure spread quickly through the school. A few hours later, Thomas left me a voicemail:

"Hi. I hope you're well... although I suspect you're not too well. I heard about your departure. I'd really like to see you again before you head down south... That is, if you want me to. Take care of yourself."

I agreed to see him one last time at my place, two days before my departure. Early in the evening, we discover that President Emmanuel Macron has announced the start of a lockdown. A disease is spreading around the world.

We continue our evening without giving it another thought. Thomas prepares dinner while I set the table. We listen to music and open a bottle of white wine. It's the first time I've shared dinner with someone in this apartment.

Despite the absence of *The Voice,* the meal is difficult. I feel like I need more and more to feel satisfied. I find it hard to concentrate on our discussions.

Fortunately, we soon move on after dinner. Thomas suggests we start a live model session. I've never had the chance to do this with someone I know. I draw him first. My felt-tip glides over the paper with difficulty. I avoid his hands, but spend a long time on his face, which I love tracing. I really enjoy this exercise. We time ourselves to work on the efficiency of the gesture. Then it's Thomas' turn to draw me. Silence settles in, disturbed only by the pencil rubbing against the paper. As he hands me his drawing, I scrutinize the rounded curves of my body, drawn in black and white. I feel beautiful in his eyes.

Unfortunately, *The Voice* suddenly reappears, ready to shatter the moment. *Your waist isn't as pronounced as it used to be, I can tell from this drawing.* This time, however, *she* doesn't manage to get the upper hand. I manage to persuade myself that feminine curves have an undeniable charm, and I stay in the moment.

Saying goodbye to Thomas is difficult. But I'm glad to have seen him again before leaving Paris.

*

Two days later, the big departure. I grab the handle of my suitcase and head for the Gare Montparnasse. I'm late and get lost in the crowd. Travelers are bustling and jostling. I can't see the train board.

Suddenly, two hands are placed over my eyes. I turn quickly, not even having time to be frightened. It's Thomas. I realize he asked me what time I was leaving the other night.

It's the most wonderful surprise. I'm moved.

Thomas pulls my suitcase to the last carriage, then waves from the platform as the train pulls away. His silhouette disappears in seconds. My heart sinks.

I hope I'll see him again one day.

Confinement

MARCH 2020, AGE 19

As soon as I get back to my parents, I step on the scales: 54 kg. My head stays down, in shock, no more emotions flowing through me. Back to my original weight, after years of struggling to stay slim. I don't recognize myself anymore.

The first Covid-19 confinement begins. My whole family is together in my childhood home. Despite the unease that accompanies me, I'm happy to be here. After years of isolation, I return to the family table and rediscover the joy of laughing with my loved ones over a good meal. I don't realize that I've found my place again in this central event of everyday life.

As the days go by, I renew my ties with my brothers. Every laugh, every discussion, every friendly exchange with them gives me the impression of reconnecting with the child I was before the illness.

During meals with my family, I eat large quantities of bread and cheese, and help myself to large portions of every dish my mother prepares. I'm happy to taste her cooking again—so many delicious dishes that take me back to my childhood memories. I take advantage of *The Voice*'s absence to fill up on all the foods *she's* forbidden me to eat over the years. I'm constantly snacking outside of mealtimes, trying out new pastry recipes, preparing hearty breakfasts laden with brioches, jams and chocolate cereals.

My body is changing at a frightening rate. In the space of six months, I put on almost 20 kg—going from 50 to 70. That's a difference of exactly 32 kg from my hospital entrance weight.

I don't recognize my silhouette any more and have trouble finding my bearings in space. When I walk, my hips bump everywhere. My cheeks are puffy and my thighs are full of cellulite. My body now resembles that of a "strong", "resistant" person, but I still feel as fragile as before. I have the unpleasant sensation that my morphology no longer corresponds to my temperament.

I don't know what to wear anymore. My T-shirts are tight, revealing my plump belly, and my pants no longer zip up. I freeze in front of my wardrobe, unable to choose an outfit that suits me. No piece in my wardrobe fits like it used to, no cut matches this new silhouette I hate. Even my shoes seem different, too small and disproportionate to the thickness of my legs.

On my mother's advice, I make an appointment with the dietician in my village, to try and ease my relationship with my body and my diet. I particularly like this woman, with whom I have long discussions. I have the impression that she understands my every word. The nutritional plans she proposes give me a framework. Unfortunately, I don't always manage to stick to them.

I sometimes feel ashamed when I go to follow-up appointments and find I've put on weight.

In the midst of my confinement, I blow out the candles of my 20th birthday and get my period back. After eight years of amenorrhea. I'm a little relieved to hear this news, as I hope to have children one day. I think back to all those nights when I prayed, with *The Voice,* to find them.

*

I spend the summer following the confinement with a group of boys from my first college. Louis, with whom I'd been chatting on my return from hospital, is one of them. I take part in many outings and parties with them, rediscovering the innocence I'd lost for so many years. With them, I laugh for hours, I let myself go, I feel understood and listened to. They take me everywhere in their cars, and gradually heal the deep wounds that *The Voice* has left me. Julien, one of the boys in the group, takes me under his wing. He's with me every step of the way, helping me discover the joys of young adulthood without ever judging me.

Unfortunately, my physical complexes hold me back in these moments of happiness. I suffer when I get ready to face the mirror before going out. I decline certain outings when I've had a major eating crisis. I don't dare bathe in front of them. I can't stand my face and body in every group photo.

Yet, strangely, I feel more desirable than before in the eyes of the men I meet. It's a very pleasant feeling that gives me self-confidence.

*

Ever since I left the École Estienne, I've had an idea for a new career. I'd like to become a tattoo artist. This goal has been with me for months. I work tirelessly, day and night, to achieve it.

Since I've had my hip tattooed, I feel differently about my body. I'm no longer focused on reshaping certain areas of my body through sport or diet, but on decorating them with new pieces. Each new tattoo engraved in my skin helps me to reappropriate my image a little more.

The impact of my first tattoos was such that I feel the need to immerse myself in this world. I hope that one day I'll be able to help others to reclaim their bodies in the same way.

To try and get an apprenticeship, I have to put together a portfolio of tattoo designs, in a coherent and impactful style. Thomas noticed that I was moving in this direction, through the drawings I regularly post on social networks. He kindly offered to give me regular advice to help me achieve my goal.

My parents, as always, encourage me in my chosen path.

After months of hard work, I began an apprenticeship on the Landes coast. But nothing turned out as I'd hoped. The boss made advances on me on the very first evening, and I didn't feel safe in the workplace.

So Thomas suggested I join him in Toulouse, his home town, where he'd been living since finishing his course at the École Estienne.

Toulouse

September 2020, Age 20

Sitting on the train to Toulouse, I watch the golden fields pass before my eyes. My stomach tightens as the terminus approaches. I'm dreading the reunion with Thomas. I hope I'll feel at ease in his environment, that everything will go smoothly and that I'll finally feel at home here.

As the train pulls into Toulouse station, I discover unique buildings unlike anything I've ever seen before. I marvel at the slightly faded orange hues, which blend perfectly with the intensity of the blue sky.

I slip my headphones over my ears, turn up the music and join the stream of travelers, all of whom seem to know their way around perfectly.

Fifteen minutes into the walk, I spot Thomas' silhouette in the distance.

I'm so happy to have him back.

*

Thomas offers to let me stay with him for a few days. Every morning, when he goes to work at the tattoo parlour, I rush to the supermarkets and bakeries. I run down the seven flights of stairs to the local supermarket. As I pass through the automatic door, I'm drawn in by the scent of industrial baguettes, fresh from the oven. My eyes widen at the temptation. I wander through the aisles, arms full of sweet goods. On the street, I hurry along, emptying wrapper after wrapper. I feel dirty. Fat. Repulsive. I walk with my eyes downcast so as not to meet anyone's gaze.

One evening, in tears, I break down and describe the course of my crises to Thomas. The donuts I eat before going to the restaurant, the bags full of pastries. He listens attentively and reassures me, without any judgment. I can't believe I dared tell him all this.

One evening, after dinner, Thomas asks me if I'd like to get together. I accepted without hesitation, tears welling up in the corners of my eyes. The fact that Thomas loves me the same way, at 45 and 70 kg, moves me deeply. A new chapter begins.

My parents, always supportive, help me move to Toulouse.

As the food crises never stop, Thomas gives me a little cuddly toy that I can slip into my pocket when I go shopping.

"It's like I'm there with you," he says.

Little by little, I manage to control some of my impulses.

Sometimes, when I panic during meals and can't make a decision, he takes my hands in his and says:

"I'm your dietician, trust me. You're allowed to eat this, it's even recommended if you want to feel good about yourself!"

Thomas is resourceful. He's an excellent cook, with a wide variety of technical dishes. At his side, I learn to prepare new, healthy and delicious recipes.

Sometimes he lends me his clothes, because I still don't know how to dress this new body of mine. I regularly slip on his pants, which are far too long and wide for me, and tie them firmly at the waist with a belt.

A month into our relationship, the second confinement begins. I get scared. I fear that the distance will separate us once again. Fortunately, Thomas's family agrees to take us both in for several weeks. Thomas's parents are very kind and welcoming. His mother cooks deliciously well—she's the one who taught Thomas to cook. I enjoy eating every meal she prepares for us, sitting at the table with her family.

*

Back in Toulouse, the food crises return with a vengeance. Fortunately, I spend some time in the tattoo parlour where Thomas works. The lively, friendly atmosphere keeps me from isolating myself, and takes my mind off certain compulsions. I love the atmosphere of this tattoo parlour. The walls are covered with drawings and paintings. Music livens up every moment. I observe every detail with an amazed eye.

It's here that I meet Jb, the salon owner who trained Thomas and later became his co-manager and friend.

Since my arrival in Toulouse, I've been working on a new, more accomplished tattoo portfolio, which may give me a better chance of getting into a salon in this city—where the level and competition are very high. Each drawing takes me days. I put all my heart into it, aware that my professional future depends on it.

When I'm drawing at the show, Jb sometimes says to me, with a smile:

"You mustn't ask for your apprenticeship anywhere else."

Thomas and I talk at length about the possibility of working together and, after careful consideration, I apply for an apprenticeship at La Zone d'Ombre, the salon Jb founded. I arrive at the salon one morning with my heart pounding, my portfolio finished and my paintings neatly packed. Jb gives me a very stressful interview. But I pull through, and he agrees to let me join the team.

Jb is an important person for me, a new member of my family, who gave me a chance and took me under his wing at a key moment in my life.

I've been working at La Zone d'Ombre for four years now, alongside him, Thomas and four other friends.

*

I'm 25 today. The five years I've spent in Toulouse have come thick and fast. I've made a lot of friends, with whom I've continued to make up for lost time. As soon as I arrived in this city, I felt the need to start a new life from scratch, surrounded by people who hadn't known me ill. This period enabled me to rebuild my life and gradually reunite with my family in better conditions.

My relationship with food and my body has calmed down over the years, but it remains complicated at times. It's difficult for me to describe exactly what I'm going through today, as I don't have enough hindsight, but I can tell you that eating disorders no longer prevent me from fulfilling my social, family and professional life. They also no longer have an impact on my health.

Following the peak of my hyperphagia (Paris/confinement/beginning of Toulouse), I alternated between periods of restriction—when *The Voice* was once again present—and food cravings. These phases have gradually smoothed out over the last three years or so. My weight has finally stabilized at 65 kg. I'm finding a balance and feeling better and better about myself. I'm much less obsessed with food than I used to be.

Despite all these advances, I still sometimes feel the need to use somewhat superstitious stratagems to maintain the pleasure of eating socially, without going to extremes of compulsion or restriction. For example, I eat only three items per bowl in an aperitif tray, so as not to lose track of the quantities I take in during the excitement of a party or family gathering. As I no longer weigh my food, I pay close attention to the plate I serve myself at the start of the meal: it has to appear visually balanced at first glance, so that I can eat it with complete peace of mind. In most cases, there's nothing to worry about, and I can continue eating naturally.

The technique that is now most present in my relationship with food is the following: I try to listen to my hunger and my body's needs and desires every day. This technique, which is very natural for some people, is very difficult to apply for people with eating disorders.

As far as anorexia nervosa is concerned—which is the eating disorder I suffered from for the greatest number of years—it calmed down the day I was able to respond to *The Voice* Within, to defend myself against what *She* was imposing on me, to reason with myself about certain situations, which may have seemed simple on the outside, but which *She* was blinding me to. Finding the strength to question this inner "voice" on my own took an enormous amount of time, patience and hard work. Even today, with my physical health restored and my mental equilibrium improved, I can still find myself at a loss when *She* resurfaces.

In my professional life, for example, I thrive every day, but the rigors imposed by *The Voice* sometimes continue to have an impact on me. I'm often too demanding of myself when it comes to my drawing and tattooing techniques.

But, fortunately, this doesn't spoil my daily life as a tattoo artist, which is both stimulating and joyful. My customers entrust me with superb projects, we do many tattoos in collaboration with Thomas and share precious moments of friendship, outside the salon, with the six members of my team.

My parents both wanted me to tattoo them right from the start. At first, I didn't dare take the plunge, because it scared me too much and I was setting the bar too high. But this year, at last, I found the courage to tattoo my father. That moment, and the trust he placed in me, touched me deeply. One day, I'll find the courage to tattoo my mother.

As for the tattoos that are multiplying on my own skin, they're always a way for me to see my body from a different angle and boost my self-confidence.

I sometimes miss *The Voice* and the darkness today. Some days, I listen to music that makes me think of *Her*. When things are really bad, *She* visits me. Her laws still inhabit me sometimes, but much more faintly than before.

Fortunately, since *The Voice* moved away from me in Paris, *She* has never had a major impact on my life.

For five years now, I've been vacationing freely with my friends and Thomas—we both realized my dream of traveling around Japan by train and bike. I party with my friends, sometimes with my brothers. I go to concerts with my dad. I walk in the forest with my mother, without being exhausted like I used to be. I share wonderful meals with my family, in-laws, Thomas and friends, without worrying about the menu.

These moments of ordinary life are a huge victory for me.

I feel better today, in the world of the living.

Afterwords

Professional Viewpoints

Doctor Alice Letessier, psychiatrist

Your weapons and our care

I remember, Oihana, your frail figure entering the consulting room, blue eyes hollowed out, pale complexion tired, thin lips purplish, your body wrapped up in the vice of anorexia.

As with all these young patients, the disease had already worked hard to make you believe that happiness lay in thinness.

This pathological thinness is only the visible part of a mysterious and complex disorder that medicine and psychiatry have difficulty understanding and treating...

Anorexia nervosa is one of the eating disorders. It also includes binge eating disorder and bulimia nervosa.

These disorders are listed in the DSM 5, the Diagnostic Manual of Mental Disorders.

Oihana, you describe perfectly the insidious process of taking control to combat the anguish of body change linked to puberty, coupled with the anxiety of disappointing and no longer being the one who fulfills all parental desires.

The body becomes the object of this control, because it no longer obeys the ideals, it has formed, and therefore deformed, it has put on weight, and this is unbearable.

Anorexia nervosa mainly affects girls (nine girls for every boy) between the ages of 14 and 19.

The incidence of this disorder has been more or less stable since the 1970s, at around 1% of the female population. Since the 2000s, we've seen a rejuvenation of anorexia nervosa, which can affect girls as young as 10 or 11, i.e. before puberty.

What used to affect teenage girls on the verge of turning 18 and taking their A-levels can now be seen in schoolgirls and impubescent girls...

This disease is also characterized by social and societal factors, with an increased risk in affluent socio-professional circles. A feature of Western, industrialized, consumerist societies, where abundance, individualism and competition are the new paradigms and other values that have become dogmas. Even as educational models.

However, history reveals that this disease has always existed. Depending on the era, biases of understanding have varied.

In the Middle Ages, "mystical anorexia" testified either to the intervention of a supernatural being, diabolical possession or a divine miracle. Young girls, most often peasants, dedicated themselves to ascetic reclusion within a church, illustrating the religious myth of inedia (life without food for several years).

Fasting often plays a role in different religions, which is biologically explained by adaptive changes in the body and psyche. Anyone who has ever experienced fasting has observed an improvement in well-being, an elation of mood, a feeling of lightness and enhanced intellectual acuity.

Some cases have been studied thanks to hagiography: Elisabeth of Hungary in the 13th century, Catherine of Siena in the 14th century, Marie de l'Incarnation in the 17th century, Thérèse de Lisieux and Simone Weil in the 19th century.

At the beginning of the 19th century, thanks to advances in science and medicine, anorexia was perceived in a more hygienic and biological light, "chlorosis" specifically in young, noble and beautiful virgins... At the end of the 19th century, this mysterious consumption was perceived as hysteria, *anorexia nervosa,* by a nascent psychiatry.

At the beginning of the 20th century, psychoanalysis opened up a field of reflection on the mother/daughter bond, the rejection of sexuality and motherhood...

The post-Second World War period and the Trente Glorieuses saw an upsurge in the incidence of this pathology, which was recognized as a mental illness and classified in the various DSMs.

Psychiatry began to take an interest in the condition, offering care and treatment options, with the creation of specialized centers in the 1980s. Creation of a national network, then a Federation, FFAB (Fédération Française Anorexie Boulimie).

Let's come back to you, Oihana, at the age of 12, you don't like your body anymore, you don't recognize it and your fears of not measuring up are gaining ground.

The transformation of a child's body into the imperfect body of an adolescent requires work that can be painful and distressing. It's a question of loss: loss of identity, of place, of sensations, of looks... for a space-time unknown. Body space and psychic time become distorted...

In the 2010s, the societal injunctions of beauty, youth and slimness are raging, and the identification models essential to the development of every teenager show aesthetic ideals in a reconditioned plastic... unattainable. Plastic without humanity.

How can we weather this storm, which attacks from within and without? How do we keep control so as not to collapse, so as not to lose face?

A few kilos less, and all will be well.

The vicious circle of addiction sets in, with eating disorders now recognized as an addiction, a drug without substance, a drug of control for the intoxication of lack.

Restriction becomes a victory, a success over oneself and over the basic need for food, which explains the denial of disorders, very frequent in the beginning: why change what works? Why change what works? What gives value and a sense of well-being?

The relationship with food is not the only symptom; other behaviors or thoughts invade the personality.

Obsession with calories, recipes, dieting, rites and rituals, OCD, purging behaviors, physical hyperactivity, standing, potomania, dysmorphophobia, grossophobia...

Psychologically, irritability, susceptibility, perfectionism, hyper-intellectualization, sleep disorders, then withdrawal, social isolation with emotional anesthesia.

When should you be concerned? When should you seek help?

When weight loss becomes too great and/or too rapid, a consultation with the attending physician is essential. Parents, as guarantors of their child's health, can seek advice from their GP.

Depending on the child's clinical condition, this doctor will refer the child to a specialist if necessary.

This pathology requires a dual approach, both somatic and psychological.

The body can adapt to the restriction for a very long time, but there is a vital limit, making it one of the few fatal psychiatric illnesses. 5-10% of patients die, either from somatic complications or suicide. Early treatment is a protective factor (lower mortality).

Care hurts, you describe it well, Oihana. I'd so much like to be able to prescribe the pill that, miraculously, in just a few days of treatment, would remove the octopus, *The Voice, She,* installed in the depths of the patient's psyche.

Like a malevolent and destructive co-pilot who has taken control, you, Oihana, and so many others have been stripped of your pilot's seat, this co-pilot lies to you and plays on your suffering, doubts and fears, the better to grow in your place.

Medical-psychological care accompanies the patient's struggle, proposing solutions, but the keys are obscure. The parent/child and caregiver/caregiver bond, as well as communication in a climate of trust, are the main tools.

A few medicinal crutches also contribute to recovery, despite the fear that they may make you fatter!

I agree with you Oihana, your parents were patient, attentive, unconditional and loving in supporting your evolution and, above all, your choices. Your current self-fulfilment is surely the greatest reward for fighting alongside you.

Not all patients with eating disorders go through the difficult ordeal of hospitalization, but in the most severe cases, with undernutrition, malaise, asthenia and metabolic disorders, hospitalization is essential.

You have to nourish a body that can't take it anymore, that's exhausted, that's falling down...

Yes, the nasogastric tube is useful, like a new umbilical cord connected to the mother's perf...

A malnourished brain becomes depressed, suffers, and can no longer produce rational, positive, calming thoughts.

Renutrition helps us to think clearly and correctly, just as much as it helps us to regain physical energy.

Nutritional intake is the *sine qua non* of recovery, and then of healing, but the enemy, lurking in the solitude of a hospital room, won't let go, and the battle against calories and the fear of putting on weight can be very long.

Anorexia can evolve over several years—two years for the simplest cases, four years more often.

But some patients develop a chronic disorder, where weight remains insufficient, thin, but stable and without danger. A professional, family, sexual and emotional life is possible, and control is required, but compatible with a normal life.

Sometimes, anorexia reveals a more severe psychiatric pathology, such as schizophrenia, bipolar disorder, *borderline* disorder or post-traumatic syndrome. Around 30% of patients who develop anorexia/bulimia have been sexually abused as children.

Psychological care requires more extensive treatment, medication and comprehensive care.

Psychological support is essential, for both patients and parents. Family therapy is recommended to move forward together and untie knots that sometimes go back to previous generations.

Understanding the disease, identifying the enemy, adopting supportive behaviours and finding the strength to exist without *her*.

When the stranglehold loosens, the great fear becomes bulimia... Another facet of ADD that often lies dormant beneath anorexia and awakens when hunger returns, when the pleasure of eating invites itself to the bakery...

A response to long restriction, lack and deprivation? But above all, a shameful, guilt-ridden turn, a degrading and unbearable loss of control with its corollary, weight gain.

In this difficult phase of the evolution of certain restrictive anorexias, a patient once told me: *"I won't have the strength to be anorexic any more"*, or another: *"Anorexia is the only thing I've achieved"*.

Your path through hyperphagia, Oihana, also testifies to the great complexity of these disorders, their painful evolution and the daily efforts to develop calming strategies.

Anorexia nervosa acts as an antidepressant, providing protection, reassurance and a positive self-image at a time of identity doubt, anguish and suffering common in adolescence. It even has the gift of appropriating identity... Isn't it common to say: "She's an anorexic"? Or even among patients: "I am anorexic"? An abuse of language! How can it be an illness? In fact, medicine and psychiatry still have some way to go. We still say: "He's schizophrenic", "She's bipolar"... No! "They suffer from..." "They have a...". That's better, isn't it?

When the antidepressant stops, another period of suffering may set in, but not systematically. Binge eating is not a failure, but a new stage in the battle, a second half.

Other questions and other needs for accompaniment and support.

Behind every eating disorder or symptom lies a person, a unique personality, admittedly fragile and weakened by the disease, but eager to exist for itself and find its place.

Your great artistic talent, Oihana, quickly dazzled us at the Maison des Adolescents. The finesse and precision of your features in depicting this young girl "Who just wanted to fly" enables us to guide and reassure patients on their road to recovery.

They recognize themselves, find support for optimism and projection into the future.

For the fundamental question, when illness tends to fade away, is: "Who am I if I'm cured? Who am I without *her*?

As caregivers, we need to help people let go of the "comfort" of a disorder that accompanies them, that brings them the attention of those around them, that makes them feel valued. A *friend,* as patients sometimes call her...

It's a long-term process, all the way to rebirth.

Thank you so much, Oihana, for having the courage and sincerity to reveal yourself, your torments, your struggles and now your energy and hopes.

It's up to us to listen to them, to understand them without judgement. Illness is not a fault, we don't choose to be ill.

But I tend to believe that patients have a choice of ways to recover.

Doctor Virginie Robert, hospital pediatrician at the Maison des Adolescents

Anorexia nervosa is the illness that disrupted Oihana's childhood and adolescence.

Eating disorders, including anorexia and bulimia, are now a public health emergency: they are the second leading cause of death in the 15-24 age group, after road accidents.

By 2025, nearly a million people in France will be affected, mostly but not exclusively girls. These disorders occur during a key period in life, when adolescents are growing up, and combine somatic and psychiatric emergencies.

And yet, this pathology remains mysterious, confidential and difficult to prevent and detect.

For seventeen years now, I've been accompanying these young patients in consultations at the Maison des Adolescents and in the pediatric ward at Pau Hospital. I can testify to the battle they wage against irrational thoughts, against a pernicious disease that leads them to believe they are in control, when in fact they are under its grip.

The symptoms and clinical signs of anorexia nervosa are often caricatural, and we know how to spot them even before the teenager is aware of her illness. This helps us in the consultation to show them that we understand what they're going through, but in reality, every presentation is atypical. We have to come to terms with each person's personality and particular history, and with an illness that will never cease to oppose care.

When a decision is taken to hospitalize a patient, most often to set up an urgent renutrition program, the reactions of the girls in my care oscillate between anger and relief. They struggle, but are no longer alone.

My job as a paediatrician is first and foremost to nourish the brain and give it the energy to fight the psychological symptoms, but this is a stage at risk of major decompensation, which mobilizes the hospital team for weeks on end and leaves both patient and family in a bad way.

We work closely with our patients over long periods, and in my department, each care project is discussed by a multidisciplinary pediatric and child psychiatric team. We know that illness is always on the lookout for loopholes in our decisions as caregivers, to justify why we can't win the battle. That's why we need to be constantly vigilant, and to break down the divisions between patient-family-caregivers imposed by the disease. I'm convinced that this cohesion is our strength against the symptoms.

Our young patients often arrive in hospital locked in a body without feelings. Their senses are, in their words, anaesthetized: the sight of a dish no longer whets the appetite, the smell of a food disgusts, the texture repels... The disease will render life insipid and unappealing. Oihana clearly described the eating rituals and the very neutral types of food that made up her meals. To heal, we need to re-educate our senses, and let go of our hold on food, so that the body can reappropriate the function of eating. But not being anaesthetized is perhaps also what revives certain pains...

Testimonials like Oihana's are invaluable: they help us, as carers of teenagers, to understand how we grow up with illness.

It's also an interesting insight into the experience of care. We imagine their suffering, but we don't experience it.

Some patients tell us, once they've recovered, that the hardest part of the early stages of the disease is resisting the hunger pangs. How can you imagine doing that to yourself when you've just left childhood behind?

Others hardly dare testify to the voice that compels them day and night.

The doctor's role is to rationalize irrational thoughts: a malnourished brain, without sufficient caloric intake, will hallucinate. This is a well-known neuroscientific mechanism.

A malnourished body will see itself as too fat, yes, that's a reality for a malnourished brain.

To feel nothing when you lose weight, to be detached from your bodily perceptions, is quite classic; it's not a particular point, but a known evolution of the disease.

This battle against oneself is the worst kind of imprisonment, and even bedridden in a hospital room, patients testify to a far worse imprisonment, that inside their own bodies.

They build and grow through their illness...

Anorexia nervosa is a chronic, long-lasting illness, with improvements followed by relapses... but yes, it can be cured, and you in turn can bear witness to help others.

Oihana left me her drawings in a booklet several years ago. Her illustrations often help me interact with teenagers during long hospital stays for renutrition.

Thank you, Oihana, for writing your story, thank you for sharing your strength, thank you for helping us understand a little better what you've been through. Your testimony is important for all of us.

Appendices

1. My Return to Anorexia

Advice and Reflections

It's been five years now since I moved away from eating disorders. I say "away" because I've retained some of the fragility and after-effects of those years of anorexia/bulimia/hyperphagia.

Despite these minor difficulties, I'm much better today and lead my life forgetting, some days, that eating disorders punctuated my life for eight years.

Anorexia nervosa is a complex illness that results from a combination of various factors: personal, family, societal...

In my view, it can occur at a time of upheaval and/or emotional fragility, when the person concerned is seeking to protect him or herself through control and the establishment of reassuring reference points.

For me, anorexia was a way of clinging to my childhood, at the dawn of adolescence, through a slim body and a fusional relationship with my parents. In this way, I delayed my fear of change a little longer.

The desire to match the valorized standard of femininity in the 1990s-2010s was also closely linked to the development of my anorexia.

However, my experience as a young teenager by no means represents the entirety of people with eating disorders. It's essential to remember that these mental illnesses can occur at any age, in people of all genders and from all walks of life. Each person's journey is unique.

Based on my personal experience, I still feel a great deal of anger towards certain aspects of society that I believe are partly responsible for the increase in certain eating disorders in recent decades:

- the public figures who promoted extreme thinness in the years 1990-2010, on TV and elsewhere;
- coaches of certain sports—such as dance, gymnastics, athletics and many others—who forced their students to lose weight under the pretext of performance;
- certain fashion designers, who treat models like articulated puppets;
- advertisements, beauty contests and TV shows that promote a certain type of physique—limited to a specific weight, age and height;
- pre-summer diet magazines—these are on display for children in supermarkets, instilling injunctions and complexes from an early age;

- certain famous doll brands, whose unrealistic bodies and lack of inclusivity were, until very late in life, presented as a model of beauty;
- finally, individuals of all generations, who are constantly criticizing and comparing each other's bodies.

But it's important to point out that anorexia is not limited to the above-mentioned societal causes; it can also arise as a result of trauma, physical and psychological abuse and violence, bereavement, harassment, intense stress and so on.

As for theories that place the mother as solely responsible for the development of anorexia nervosa, I find them generalizing and unfounded in most cases. In my case, for example, my mother was not THE reason for my downfall. Anorexia nervosa is much more complex than that. It's easy and dangerous to jump to conclusions that make you feel guilty.

Even if anorexia nervosa can be explained by certain concrete reasons, it will always retain certain mysteries for me. It's an obscure journey, on the edge of death, that brings together people from different walks of life, yet whose actions and thoughts are often similar. In my opinion, these similarities reinforce the idea that "anorexic" behavior is hardly under the control of the people concerned.

I'd like to emphasize an important point here. Many people consider anorexia nervosa to be a "whim", but it's not: sufferers go through immense pain, losing contact with loved ones and precious moments in their lives. No one would wish to inflict such suffering on themselves voluntarily. There's no point, no pleasure, no choice.

To come back to my treatment, I may have fallen ill at home, but the psychiatric hospital I was admitted to did nothing for me.

Rather, it was the source of certain traumas in my subsequent development, due to the inordinate confinement, the complete estrangement from loved ones and the constant mistrust of the nursing staff towards people with anorexia/bulimia.

Institutions specializing in eating disorders may have evolved in recent years, but I can't vouch for that.

My negative experience is limited to one psychiatric hospital, but the Maison des Adolescents, which accompanied me for several years, was a great help.

*

Finally, I have a few words of advice for people suffering from anorexia nervosa: never stop believing in your dreams, and be as indulgent as possible with yourself. You didn't choose to fall into this illness; you'd probably rather be free and happy. So don't make those around you feel guilty. You're going through a serious illness and are doing your best to survive.

Never give up hope, always remember that the human brain is complex and wonderful, and that nothing is irreversible. Take the time to face one step at a time, when you feel able. Don't pay attention to the clumsiness of people you meet along the way. In most cases, it's not malicious.

Anorexia doesn't define you. You'll get over it sooner or later. The road to recovery may be long, but this ordeal will help make you a wonderful person.

Here's some advice for the loved ones of people with anorexia/bulimia: try to be as indulgent as possible towards your loved one who's going through a difficult period, as well as towards yourself. It's normal to lose patience when you're too scared and tired: don't feel guilty. Always remember that people with anorexia nervosa are dealing with an inner conflict that demands their full attention. It will be very difficult for them to apply your advice, despite their good will. They are in great pain and need tenderness and understanding. Try to open a dialogue with them, to understand what's going on in their heads. Orders will only accentuate their inner conflict. After difficult meals, try to be supportive.

If they start to gain weight again, be discreet and normalizing. Compliment her beauty if you feel it makes her feel better, but don't comment on her figure or body parts. That would be too risky and could inadvertently arouse insecurity in her, no matter what adjective you use.

Team up, don't be too hard on yourself and keep hope alive.

2. Words from my Parents

Finally, I asked my parents to write a text containing their feelings about this period, and advice for those close to people with eating disorders.

Here's my father's.

"These eight years have been like a tunnel that suddenly engulfs you in the very difficulty of life...

The soft light of ordinary life is extinguished and anguish takes hold of you for good.

At first, you quickly realize that it's really very serious, even if you start dreaming that it won't be and that there will be ways out.

As for me, I'll never stop hoping that things will get better the next day.

That's probably what kept me going for so long...

As with all misfortunes in life, we tell ourselves that 'it's not possible,' that it's not going to happen to us when everything seemed to be going so well...

In fact, it all happens very quickly, and even if we warn you by saying 'you know, be very careful, you could 'fall' into anorexia!' it's already too late, the mental disorder has already set in and taken over...

I won't go back over the many causes that Oihana describes so well, but I'll simply try to give some advice to parents who might find themselves caught up in this whirlwind.

The first of these 'tips' is for me the most important. It's about not breaking the link with your child, making a clear distinction between the 'illness' that has taken over his personality, and your child himself, who is still there, totally lost and distraught, even if the way he acts suggests that he's dominating the situation 'his way', with a logic that's totally beyond you!

It's important to understand that the hold is total and that, as long as the illness is present, your child will no longer be the person he was just a few days ago...

It's very difficult to understand and accept this!

It's a mental illness that's going to change everything.

The 'voice' that orders is stronger than anything. No matter how many hours you spend trying to reason with your child, it (the voice) will have the last word. It's important to be aware of this, and above all not to hold it against your child, who is suffering as much as you are.

Of course, you can expect to hear comments from family and friends, or from professionals, such as:

'I wouldn't do it like that! A good slap, a good kick up the backside and, believe me, my daughter would eat her plate!'

If it were that simple, disease wouldn't exist...

Of course, this type of exchange will keep you away from this type of person, who is fortunately in the minority. Your child is in mortal danger, and your own equilibrium is extremely precarious at this very moment. You discover a strength you never knew you had... But you don't need to hear that!

For my part, I continued to work normally without taking a single day off, certainly to pretend that it wasn't so serious and that things would soon be much better.

For the most part, I've continued to smile and laugh even in my professional environment, with a few 'cracks' (bursting into tears) in small groups with my close and trusted colleagues... I'd like to take this opportunity to thank them for having been my crutches all these years!

The second piece of advice is to accept that you're not perfect in this situation.

Inevitably, you'll break down, as I did myself, you'll get carried away, your words will go beyond your thoughts, because the situation will inevitably impose it...

But you too will have the right to make mistakes, because stress, fatigue and even exhaustion will lead you to lose control.

All you have to do is talk about it, express your regrets and your legitimate helplessness! The whole family will be affected (brothers and sisters too, as you'll inevitably have less time and attention to give them) and we'll all have to manage 'the crisis' together, without knowing for how many days, weeks, months, years...

So, my last piece of advice is to encourage any improvement, however small, and above all to support any project expressed for the future...

Don't hesitate to take risks, even if the project seems unattainable under current conditions. The important thing is to imagine a better future and to do everything possible to move towards it...

Any positive change is to be encouraged; it's all about giving life back its 'taste', no pun intended...

Oihana often told me that she didn't want to leave childhood behind, that 'it was so good before', that she had no desire to become an adult like the rest of us with professional worries (gosh, yet another reason to feel guilty, I've certainly shared too many of my difficulties and doubts!

Of course, you can still feel guilty and say to yourself what a disastrous image I've given of adulthood!

But we mustn't forget that it's certainly the 'voice' that still governs and finds every possible stratagem to achieve its ends...

You're no more 'bad parents' than your friends, you do the best you can, and if your child tells you he or she doesn't want to leave childhood behind, because it was too good... well, at least you've succeeded in giving your child a happy childhood!

The interpretation that is made afterwards is totally created by the illness.

For my part, and in response to this, I told her that she could relive those wonderful moments when she had children of her own. The idea is to give perspective, to keep hope alive for the future!

As for medical care, it was very uneven…

As in all walks of life, professional or otherwise, you can encounter the best as well as the worst.

As grateful as I am to the professionals at the Maison des Adolescents and the hospital in Pau (wonderful nurses in the vast majority of cases) (I'd like to take this opportunity to salute them and thank them warmly), I still have 'very serious reservations' about psychiatric care.

I'd like to take direct aim at Mme Brisset (as Oihana calls her), who was particularly nasty to me.

Two murderous sentences (recounted in Oihana's text), one on entering, the other on leaving, as if to finish the job!

I arrived with complete confidence, certain of being supported and even understood by 'specialists,' but I found just the opposite. Adding guilt to the shoulders of parents who are already fragile and sinking—you can imagine that coming from people who are far removed from these issues and devoid of basic empathy! But coming from professionals, I think it's a mistake, an uppercut to a person who's already ashore and trying to keep his head above water.

What a lack of tact and professionalism!

I'll never forgive him! I was speechless with rage inside…

My distress only became apparent when an outsider asked me what I thought of the feedback I'd received from the health professionals in this establishment, and I burst into tears. My upbringing obliges me not to criticize. I prefer to leave her alone with her conscience.

I still get teary-eyed when I talk to friends about it more than ten years later!

I must not forget to offer my sincere congratulations and thanks to the vast majority of others, including my GP.

Before concluding, I'd like to say a few words about those people, family or friends, who, with great tact and kindness, were able to adapt to the realities of our time. When it was time to sit down to dinner, knowing not to say anything when Oihana stayed in her room, and accepting her as she was, sickly sickly, with no hair on her temples, and less and less as time went by, sometimes with no filter in her words.

She never lost her smile, even if it too often turned to tears.

All these people who knew how to remain present in this emotional storm, simply by our side, supporting and loving. We thank them all!

Finally, I often used the metaphors of the light at the end of the tunnel or the famous 'you have to hit rock bottom to get to the surface'...

Well, that's it, we're in the light and we've risen to the surface, stronger than before, richer from the hard battle we had to fight and from which we emerged victorious!

So don't lose hope! And long live life!"

*

Now, here's my mother's text.

"The exercise is difficult. As I set about it, I become aware with admiration of what Oihana has achieved, trying to transform pain into words that can heal, give hope through her testimony, help to understand by showing the inside.

I arrive after the essential has been said, by Oihana with precision and delicacy and, as far as the parents are concerned, by my husband, clearly and fairly. I agree with everything. I don't think it's necessary to add more, but I'll go ahead.

Four years have gone by and I'm overwhelmed by the present. But when I try to write about this period, so many doubts and questions resurface that I can barely bear witness to what I experienced. There's bound to be some repetition of what's already been said, but that's inevitable.

It happens very quickly. You start to worry and then it's all over. It's like being in a car with no brakes, on a descent into fog. We try to understand where we are. We argue, we explain, we look for metaphors to convince us, formulas we believe to be unstoppable. We argue, we get angry, we're scared, we despair.

But it goes fast, too fast. My mother's love is worthless. I thought it would protect my children against everything. Where did we go wrong? What's my part? Trying over and over to understand the origin. I imagine it like a too-tight shoelace that you can't undo. Like the arms of an octopus. I'm probably one of those arms. What can I do about it? Every day, we try to figure out what to do. We'd love to find the phrase that makes it all click. We have children in the hope that they'll be happy, not to see them like this. That wasn't the plan. We're in a race against time, his strength is running out.

The hospital. Seeing her every lunchtime in front of her meal trays, unable to eat. Doing her hair after a shower. Handfuls of her hair left in my hands. Fighting to bring her markers, sheets of paper, a computer with games, in the hope that she'll regain a taste for life. But she sleeps a lot, a bit like a plant. She no longer has the strength for magic and drawing. To be present when the catheter is put back in and to be in her pain. Beg her to at least go out onto the patio, in the hope that the fresh air will bring her back to life.

I've heard that in Bordeaux, there's a specialized center where girls with eating difficulties are welcomed, with adapted therapies. A place where she could move forward. We live on hope. Then came the horror, nothing there, not old enough for the special group. She is confronted with traumatic situations which, it is thought, aggravate her condition. We're still fighting to be able to see her, to get her out a bit, to have at least one plant in her room. She tells us she can't stay there. That she's going to die there. Is it her talking or her 'voice' resisting change? What part of her is this (damn) voice? How do you tell the difference? What's the right choice? Who should we listen to? We make the decision. We sign the release form. Are we saving her? Are we condemning her to years of chronicity?

And she goes home. We understand the word stabilization. But it lasts. For years. Being awkward. Not finding the right words, but exchanging a lot. Looking for the best way to do it, the experience that will make her want to change. We'd love to spare her the pain. But, despite her efforts, her determination and her kindness, she's wasting away, little by little. Before our increasingly powerless eyes. How can you tell the difference between helping and supporting a disease, when your child's life is at stake?

And the Paris project. Is it really possible? We're thought to be irresponsible parents. What's the alternative? To see her shrink, to see her die out year after year? Then she fights relentlessly to make her dream come true. And it works!

Life finally takes its rightful place. She calls it. And she goes for it. With such courage. So fragile. She's making the change. Far from us. She accepts to grow, to live, to blossom, to take risks.

Like when the clouds part and the blue sky appears. It clears, little by little.

And you can breathe again.

I can't thank her enough. For fighting. For always talking to us. For hanging in there all those years. For not letting us down. For being here today.

Thank you also to each member of our family, to Thomas, to each of his friends, to each of his encounters who, from near or far, have been there, helped build his present.

And to all those who supported us, who listened to us and accompanied us in moments of despair. May love win.

Over the years, I've searched through books of personal accounts, each one more moving than the last, for the magic key that could enlighten us and make things click. In each book, I hoped to find the solution. But it's difficult, because each case is different, each parent/child relationship unique, the paths and role of chance in our incalculable lives so mysterious, and the choice to live can only come from within.

So I've just come up with a few thoughts.

I remember the first piece of advice that someone who had been through illness gave me (thank you, Géraldine, for taking the time): *Stay connected. Ease the communication.* For us, it was invaluable in ensuring that meals, which had become battlefields, stopped turning into disasters. It's not a question of avoiding conflict, but of understanding that we're not just dealing with a whim. And that, in this situation, shouting won't help.

For the more optimistic/ingenic among us, when we have children, we can believe that our love is so strong that it will always be able to protect them against everything. When we're approaching the worst, we may doubt its quality, our validity as parents. I doubted myself.

But in the end, we can love, accompany and support our children as much as we can, and life will still bring them happiness and misfortune that they'll have to face on their own.

As far as seeking medical help is concerned, it's not unusual to hear a few pithy phrases. Like when you arrive at a renowned psychiatrist's, helpless and lost in the face of so many daily choices, with very basic questions like: *when I buy a twelve-pack of low-fat yoghurt every day, am I helping my daughter or supporting her illness? What do I do when faced with the 'I'll eat this or I'll eat nothing' choice when my life depends on it?* And you're told the obvious: 'If the child has an eating disorder, since the source of the food is the mother, the origin of the eating disorder is the mother.' Leave with this, after a day's work, late after waiting three hours in a crowded waiting room. Go shopping, and have the same yoghurt again before going home.

I'm no expert. I haven't studied the causes of the trigger. I'm ready to assume my share of responsibility, all of it, if that would help in any way, but making parents feel guilty without providing the slightest usable clue in the moments when it's so important that they don't disperse their forces, doesn't help much.

So now's the time to stay strong, to keep refocusing, to sort through comments and readings. Our choices will often have to be 49/51%, so we won't have any more certainties. We can only do the best we can.

Even if it's not easy to find the right help, it does exist. As much as I've spent days scouring hospitals, medical centers, specialized services and aid associations in Paris, only to end up finding a half-hour appointment in a completely saturated CMP, we've been lucky enough to be warmly welcomed, for example, at the Maison des Adolescents in Pau, and over the years we've met psychologists, psychiatrists, nurses, secretaries, doctors, therapists, all of them caring and human.

So, it does exist. Don't be discouraged. Of course, each new search for help is difficult. It's hard on those who are at the end of their tether, but you can find support in the end.

Finally, I wouldn't dare to speak to anyone who suffers from ADD, as everyone is so unique. Just, perhaps when you can, help us, talk to us, explain to us. So that we can try to do the right thing. And let's avoid any guilt. It doesn't make sense. Nobody decides to suffer from an eating disorder.

We can get out of it. I wish you all the strength, courage and luck in the world.

Thank you, Oihana, for standing by us."

3. Acknowledgments

First of all, I'd like to thank my parents, who have been with me every step of the way during this difficult period. I love them from the bottom of my heart.

Thanks to my brothers, Unai and Peio, who have been strong, loving, supportive, accommodating and mature throughout all these years.

Thank you to all the other members of my family who have been there, each in their own way, but always with the best of wills.

Thank you to my friends who have, in turn and without realizing it, enabled me to make up for lost time and laughter.

I'd like to thank my classmates from my art school in Paris, who supported and accepted me despite the great fragility I felt during this period (Alix, Anja, Leyla, Marie-Lou, Lucas, Juliette, Adem, Martin, Zoé, Lilly); my friends from school, college and high school, who knew me at different ages and in different states, and who always welcomed me as if I'd never left (Chloé M., Chloé D., Laure, Julien, Maxence, Louis, Manon, Axelle, Diane, Lucas, Lozane); and my friends in Toulouse, who taught me that it's possible to be assertive and have fun, no matter what your body or background (Jp, Charlie, Eliot, Jb, Meli, Rubie, Paulo, Axel, Nico, Jonas, Caroll, Nono, Stéphanie, Salomé, Matteo and Rémy).

Thanks to my in-laws for their warm welcome and inspiring discussions.

Thank you to my teachers and the members of the nursing staff who believed in me (doctors, psychiatrists, psychologists, sophrologists, physiotherapists, dieticians, nurses, care assistants...). Thank you to the team at the Maison des Adolescents in Pau for their professionalism and gentleness.

Finally, thanks to my wonderful partner, Thomas, who has shared my life for nearly seven years, and who helps me every step of the way, in the best possible way.

4. Playlist

During anorexia:

Comptine d'un autre été—Yann Tiersen
¡Cuánto frío hace en Saturno!—Doctor Deseo
Palabras para Julia—Paco Ibáñez
Siempre me quedará—Bebe
Where's My Love—SYML
Waltz—Evgeny Grinko
Wasting My Young Years—London Grammar
Between the Buttons—French 79
Fine on the Outside—Priscilla Ahn
New Person, Same Old Mistakes—Tame Impala
Walzer für Niemand—Sophie Hunger
Avec le temps—Léo Ferré
Dans les steppes de l'Asie centrale—Alexandre Borodine
Infinita tristeza—Manu Chao
Mystery of Love—Sufjan Stevens
Song for Jesse—Nick Cave & Warren Ellis
Parfum Thérémine—L'Impératrice
Maggot Brain—Funkadelic
Almost Blue—Chet Baker

Table of Contents

Best sellers Max Milo Editions

The Russian Art of War, Jacques Baud

Hitler's banker, Jean-François Bouchard

Confessions of a forger, Éric Piedoie Le Tiec

The Koran and the flesh, Ludovic-Mohamed Zahed

Governing by fake news, Jacques Baud

Governing by chaos, Collectif

A political history of food, Paul Ariès

Mad in U.S.A.: The ravages of the "American model", Michel Desmurget

Mondial soccer club geopolitics, Kévin Veyssière

Putin: Game master?, Jacques Baud

Treatise on the three impostors: Moses, Jesus, Muhammad, The Spirit of Spinoza

TV Lobotomy, Michel Desmurget

www.ingramcontent.com/pod-product-compliance
Lightning Source LLC
Chambersburg PA
CBHW050525240926
51846CB00003B/694